COMBAT AIRCRAFT

134 ARADO Ar 234 BOMBER AND RECONNAISSANCE UNITS

SERIES EDITOR TONY HOLMES

134 COMBAT AIRCRAFT

Robert Forsyth and
Nick Beale

ARADO Ar 234 BOMBER AND RECONNAISSANCE UNITS

OSPREY
PUBLISHING

OSPREY PUBLISHING
Bloomsbury Publishing Plc
PO Box 883, Oxford, OX1 9PL, UK
1385 Broadway, 5th Floor, New York, NY 10018, USA
E-mail: info@ospreypublishing.com
www.ospreypublishing.com

OSPREY is a trademark of Osprey Publishing Ltd

First published in Great Britain in 2020

A catalogue record for this book is available from the British Library.

ISBN: PB: 9781472844392; eBook 9781472844408; ePDF 9781472844378; XML 9781472844385

20 21 22 23 24 10 9 8 7 6 5 4 3 2 1

Edited by Tony Holmes
Cover Artwork by Mark Postlethwaite
Aircraft Profiles by Janusz Światłoń
Index by Alan Rutter
Originated by PDQ Digital Media Solutions, UK
Printed and bound in India by Replika Press Private Ltd

Osprey Publishing supports the Woodland Trust, the UK's leading woodland conservation charity.

To find out more about our authors and books visit **www.ospreypublishing.com**. Here you will find extracts, author interviews, details of forthcoming events and the option to sign up for our newsletter.

ACKNOWLEDGMENTS

Nick Beale would like to thank Andrew Arthy, David E Brown, Eddie J Creek, Ferdinando D'Amico, Robert Forsyth, Andy Mitchell, Tomáš Poruba, J Richard Smith, Adam Thompson, Gabriele Valentini and David Wadman for their assistance in the compilation of this book. Robert Forsyth wishes to thank the following for their kind assistance with information on the operations of KG 76 – Eddie J Creek, Roger Gaemperle, J Richard Smith, Nick Beale, Dave Wadman, Ted Oliver, Martin Pegg, Steve Coates, Chris Thomas, Tom Ivie, Huib Ottens and Frithjof Ruud.

Front Cover
In the early afternoon of 26 December 1944, Leutnant Wolfgang Ziese of *Kommando Sperling* based at Rheine, in northwest Germany, was tasked with flying an observation mission over Antwerp in Ar 234B-2 Wk-Nr 140153 T9+HH to monitor V2 rocket impacts. Antwerp, the Allies' principal supply port, had been under sustained attack from V2s since October in an assault that would last until 28 March 1945. While flying over the city at an altitude of between 7000-9000 m, Ziese observed a first impact at 1307 hrs some 7.5 km south-southwest of the city centre, west of the Willebroek road. The second followed four minutes later in the angle of the Turnhout–Maas canal, 7.5 km east-northeast of the city centre. The third rocket fell at 1314 hrs, apparently at Rikevorsel, 30 km east-northeast of the city. Photographs were taken of the impact points.

Mark Postlethwaite's specially commissioned cover artwork depicts Ziese's Ar 234 as it flies over the Belgian port city shortly after the second impact on the Turnhout–Maas canal, with smoke drifting skywards

Previous Pages
Ar 234 V1 Wk-Nr 130001 TG+KB, the first prototype aircraft, is seen here at the Arado works at Brandenburg in the summer of 1943. This excellent profile view shows the initial design of take-off dolly and landing skid (*EN Archive*)

CONTENTS

CHAPTER ONE

A NEW BOMBER

The advent of a new era in Luftwaffe jet-bomber technology began in a very inconspicuous way when, on 12 March 1944, the Arado Ar 234 V9 took off from the Arado Flugzeugwerke's factory airfield at Brandenburg-Neuendorf to fly 150 km south to the Luftwaffe airfield at Alt-Lönnewitz. Ar 234 V9 Wk-Nr 130009 PH+SQ was the latest in a series of prototypes built by Arado as test-beds for a new, high-powered, high-altitude jet reconnaissance aircraft. Powered by a pair of Jumo 004B turbojets, the V9 incorporated the single-seat, all-metal monoplane design with the slim, semi-monocoque fuselage of its immediate predecessors, but it differed in one major aspect. The initial prototype Ar 234s (V1 to V8) lacked an integrated undercarriage in favour of a landing skid. For take-off, the aircraft were loaded onto jettisonable, three-wheel dollies that weighed 635 kg apiece.

The test programme for the early prototypes had commenced on 30 July 1943 with the first flight of the V1 and was relatively successful, although the V1 and V2 suffered severe damage and a fatal engine fire, respectively, during 1943 that ended their service. The V9 was the first aircraft to dispense with the take-off dolly and skid arrangement and featured a retractable tricycle undercarriage. It was the prototype for a planned new 'B' series that would function as high-speed bombers.

In circumstances similar to the operational gestation of the Messerschmitt Me 262, in the autumn of 1943, the potential of bombing capability

The clean, simple design of the Ar 234 V9 was compromised to some extent by the necessary addition of *R-Gerät* (Walter 109-500) RATO units fitted outboard of the Jumo 004 turbojets – a 250 kg bomb has been attached to each of the latter. However, the RATO units were jettisoned shortly after the aircraft left the ground during take-off, while the ordnance did little to impede performance (*EN Archive*) was something that was never far away from the minds of the *Führer*, Adolf Hitler, and the *Reichsmarschall* of the Luftwaffe, Hermann Göring. During a conference at the *Reichsluftfahrtministerium* (RLM – German Air Ministry) on 14 October, Göring had asked, 'What does the Ar 234 carry as a bomber?' Oberstleutnant Siegfried Knemeyer, the *Chef Technische Luftrüstung* in the *Abteilung Entwicklung* (Chef TLR/E – Head of Air Technical Equipment, Development Department), replied, 'Three 500 kg and normally a 3000 kg externally.' This, combined with the Arado's projected speed of 680 km/h when carrying an external load of either fuel or bombs, served to enthuse Göring. By early December, a total output of 180 Ar 234B-2s was projected by the end of 1944.

Thus it was that the Ar 234 V9 was intended as the first B-series machine, and, a short while after it landed at Alt-Lönnewitz after having been flown by Arado's Flugkapitän Johann Ubbo Janssen, it commenced a run of some 100 test flights for both the manufacturer and the Luftwaffe's *Erprobungsstelle* (test centre) at Rechlin. Knemeyer flew the aircraft on 21 and 29 March while at Rechlin, after which he reported favourably on the type. Naturally, these test flights included the fitment of bomb racks as well as the testing of automatic release equipment and the installation of two rearward-firing 20 mm MG 151/20 cannon. The cockpit was also adapted to take a *Lotfe* 7K bombsight, an autopilot and a periscope intended to improve rear vision.

On 10 April, the V9 was joined by the V10 (another B-2 prototype), this aircraft being fitted with an RF2C rear-view periscope housed in a fairing mounted above the cockpit, based on a suggestion from Oberleutnant Erich Sommer (see Chapter 2). Eventually, in the final B-2 operational bomber version, the periscope could be turned forward for assistance when making diving attacks. Despite the image in the scope being upside down, it was believed that pilots would adapt to this shortcoming when set

A wooden mock-up of the nose section of Arado's E 370 project, which would become the Ar 234, with glazing fitted. The E 370 was close to, but not the exact design of, the eventual operational Ar 234B variant's nose. The mock-up did, however, incorporate the outline for the clear vision panel in the upper forward glazing that was a feature of the Ar 234B's cockpit (*EN Archive*)

against the advantage offered of rear vision up to 60 degrees upwards and 15 degrees downwards.

Throughout the late spring and early summer of 1944, the V9 and V10 continued to engage in intensive air-testing at Rechlin, with the former aircraft being fitted with 500 kg bombs on fairings under each turbo nacelle, while in other tests a 1000 kg bomb was loaded under the fuselage. Notable figures such as the highly decorated Generalmajor Dietrich Peltz, who commanded the Luftwaffe's bombing offensive against the British Isles, inspected both aircraft at Alt-Lönnewitz on 9 May and was favourably impressed. Major Otto Behrens, *Typenbegleiter* ('Project Leader' or 'Development Coordinator') at Rechlin for the Me 262, also stated that, generally, the Ar 234 gave a 'considerably better impression' than the Messerschmitt. On 3 July Oberst Walter Storp, the *Kommodore* of *Kampfgeschwader* (KG) 76 and a recipient of the *Ritterkreuz* (Knight's Cross),

The access panel is open on the nacelle of this Jumo 004B turbojet unit believed to be fitted to Ar 234 V2 Wk-Nr 130002 DP+AW. Although the Jumo was intended as an interim powerplant while awaiting mass delivery of BMW 003 engines, it remained in service with the B-series Ar 234 for the duration of the war (*EN Archive*)

A bomber emerges – the Ar 234 V9 Wk-Nr 130009 PH+SQ was used extensively for bombing tests in 1944. It is seen here configured for maximum load flight testing with RATO units outboard of the Jumos and 500 kg bombs fitted beneath each engine nacelle (*EN Archive*)

flew the V9, noting its first-class handling, and on the 18th he flew the V10. Two days later Storp flew the V10 in formation with the V9 and engaged in mock bombing attacks. All went well, and Storp felt that the transition of bomber pilots used to flying piston-engined aircraft to the jet would present little difficulty. On 27 July, however, the V10 was destroyed when, after a belly-landing in a field, straw that had become snared in the engine caught fire.

Nevertheless, by the time of its demise, in addition to the likes of senior Luftwaffe officers such as Storp, the V10 had also served to impress none other than the *Generalluftzeugmeister*, Generalfeldmarschall Erhard Milch, who authorised increased levels of production of the Ar 234B-2. This was all well and good, but a new aircraft would need pilots to fly it, and by the late spring of 1944 the Luftwaffe bomber force was largely redundant. Its units had been disseminated across three fronts, having suffered from attrition and heavy losses during hazardous supply and ground-attack missions on the Eastern Front, during largely ineffective bombing missions over Great Britain as masterminded by Peltz, and in defensive anti-shipping missions over the Mediterranean, where German forces were fighting to retain a foothold in Italy. Furthermore, the *Kampfgeschwader* had received few replacement aircraft, little replenishment of crews and fuel, and had lost considerable cohesion as a result of various unit re-designations and consolidation.

One bomber unit to remain in northern Italy at this time was III./KG 76, which had flown more than 10,000 sorties in operations over Poland, western Europe, England, the Soviet Union, North Africa and the Mediterranean. Like most of the bomber *Gruppen*, it too had suffered from losses, and a lack of sufficiently combat-ready crews and supplies of equipment and fuel. In late May 1944, the *Gruppe*'s Ju 88A-4s, under the command of Hauptmann Wilhelm Heid, were based at Villaorba, west of Udine, where they carried out increasingly sporadic missions against Allied forces advancing from Anzio-Nettuno, Salerno and Monte Cassino.

Heid was an officer with a predominantly staff background, although he had flown more than 100 missions. There is evidence to suggest that the unit was not the happiest in terms of morale at this time, and that a number of its officers were unpopular. Whatever the case, on 25 May 1944, Heid called a meeting of his officers at Villaorba and informed them that the *Gruppe* had been recalled to Germany, with the transfer expected to commence early the following month.

Once returned, III./KG 76 would be reunited with other elements of the *Geschwader*, including the *Geschwaderstab*, presently based at Monfalcone-Ronchi, 32 km southeast of Udine. It had just seen a change in leadership when Oberstleutnant Rudolf Hallensleben was succeeded by Oberst Walter Storp. A holder of the Knight's Cross, Storp had directed operations of the Luftwaffe's Italian-based bomber *Gruppen* in the summer of 1943. He had then served briefly in the USSR as Chief of Staff of IV. *Fliegerkorps* until he was sent back to Italy to take over from Hallensleben. Then orders came in for the *Stab* to return to the Reich along with III. *Gruppe*.

Heid told his officers that once back in Germany, they would commence preparatory training for a new aircraft powered by a new form of propulsion. Indeed, this propulsion would involve engines with 'no propellers'.

This announcement was greeted with muted astonishment by the assembled officers. So it was that a small *Vorkommando* (advance detachment) was formed under the command of Hauptmann Diether Lukesch, the *Staffelkapitän* of 9./KG 76, with orders to go to Alt-Lönnewitz, in Brandenburg, some 150 km south of Berlin. The choice of Lukesch to lead the detachment was not surprising given the track record of this veteran combat airman.

Diether Lukesch was an Austrian, born in Hadersdorf-Weidlingau, near Vienna, on 15 July 1918. His initial Luftwaffe career path saw him training to become a reconnaissance pilot, and he completed courses at schools in Perleberg, Sprottau, Grossenhain and Rahmel. After further operational training with the *Fernaufklärungsgruppe des Ob.d.L* at Döberitz, and holding the rank of Leutnant, he was posted to the *Stabsstaffel* of KG 76 on 1 August 1940. He subsequently undertook bombing missions against the British Isles with this unit.

Flying Do 17s, and putting his training to good use, Lukesch was initially assigned to fly target reconnaissance and post-raid assessment missions over England. However, he later flew bombing missions in the Do 17 and Ju 88 as Technical Officer with 7./KG 76. From the commencement of Operation *Barbarossa* in the east in June 1941, Lukesch developed an impressive combat record, despite being shot down over enemy territory during the early phase of the campaign and managing to return to German lines on foot. He was awarded the *Ehrenpokal* (Honour Goblet) shortly thereafter. Subsequently, he flew many bombing missions against Soviet supply lines and facilities and survived a difficult crash-landing. Lukesch was awarded the Knight's Cross on 20 December 1941.

In June 1942 Oberleutnant Lukesch was appointed Technical Officer of III./KG 76, and on 28 September that same year he was made *Staffelkapitän* of 9./KG 76. After further operations over southern Russia, during which he was credited with sinking 12 tankers and two cargo vessels on the Volga, he was transferred with III. *Gruppe* firstly to Crete and then to Sicily. From these locations, Lukesch carried out bombing missions against enemy supply ports in Algeria, as well as targets in Libya and Tunisia. Later, in the spring of 1944, III./KG 76 was involved in day and night operations, striking Allied supply lines in Italy and targeting the Anzio–Nettuno beachhead. Lukesch and his crew were also credited with shooting down an American bomber during a night mission. He was awarded the *Eichenlaub* (Oak Leaves) to the Knight's Cross on 10 October 1944, having flown more than 400 missions.

Surprisingly, at least a part of the *Vorkommando*, including Lukesch, made the journey to Alt-Lönnewitz in a Fieseler Fi 156 *Storch* liaison aircraft. Flying into strong headwinds, it took two days for the bomber

Three of III./KG 76's senior officers photographed in Italy in the late spring of 1944, prior to the *Gruppe*'s conversion to the Ar 234. They are, from left to right, Hauptmann Diether Lukesch (*Staffelkapitän* of 9./KG 76 who would go on to command the Ar 234 *Einsatzstaffel*), Hauptmann Josef Regler (*Staffelkapitän* of 7./KG 76) and Hauptmann Wilhelm Heid, who would oversee III./KG 76's conversion to the Ar 234 (*EN Archive*)

men to reach their destination. Nevertheless, their curiosity was still high over what it was they were expected to fly.

Although Alt-Lönnewitz was subjected to Allied air attacks during 1944, comparatively, after years on forward airfields on the main battlefronts, the *Vorkommando* found conditions at the base to be quite satisfactory. The partly paved and partly grass airfield was well equipped in terms of lighting, navigational aids, accommodation, hangars, dispersals and flak defences. The day after the arrival of the III./KG 76 *Vorkommando*, Lukesch was given a tour of the Arado facilities by *Herr* Schulz, the company's works manager. When Lukesch first set his eyes upon the distinctive, tricycle-undercarriage, 'filler-covered, highly-polished aircraft with their glazed Plexiglas cockpits' the sight left him 'with the most enduring impression of my flying career'.

Heid had been correct. These aircraft lacked conventional piston engines with propellers and instead were fitted with turbojets, which promised unrivalled speed.

With Lukesch duly impressed, Schulz next took the Luftwaffe officer for a tour of the assembly halls, before offering him the chance to fly one of the new jets. An Arado was towed out from the hangar and Schulz dropped down into the cockpit through the top entry hatch while Lukesch lay across the top of the fuselage watching and listening intently to his guide's demonstration of the instruments and controls;

'I particularly observed that regulating the revolutions up to 6000 rpm was only to be undertaken with the throttle lever, taking careful note of the temperature. It was only after this rpm was reached that the rpm regulator was engaged. Moving the throttle forward too fast would have the result of overheating the turbine, starting a fire, or even causing its destruction.'

A short while later, Lukesch sat in the cockpit, went through the start procedure and carried out some roll and braking tests. Then he pulled the overhead hatch closed, applied the throttle and eased off the brakes. He found little difference in take-off (and landing) to what was experienced in the Ju 88A-4, although the fast climbing speed was notable. Lukesch was in the air for 20 minutes before landing. He then carried out three more flights, including 'an altitude flight up to 11,000 m in an – at that time – unimaginable time of 24 minutes'.

Recognising the potential in the Ar 234, Lukesch immediately began setting about deciding upon which pilots would be suitable for conversion to the jet, and also to prepare the establishment of a new *Einsatzstaffel* (Operations Squadron) that would assess the aircraft under operational conditions and in combat missions. The *Einsatzstaffel* would be drawn mainly from a cadre of 9. *Staffel* pilots, but not exclusively.

By mid-July, Oberst Storp and the *Geschwaderstab*, together with Hauptmann Heid and the rest of III./KG 76, had arrived at Alt-Lönnewitz from Italy. Simultaneously, the *Stab* II./KG 76 commanded by Major Siegfried Geisler and 5. *Staffel* came from northern France, where they had been conducting operations on the Invasion Front. After an initial plan to switch to the Ju 188 and Me 410, I./KG 76 had also been slated to convert to the Ar 234, but after relinquishing its few remaining Ju 88s in Italy in May 1944, the *Gruppe* returned firstly to Hörsching and then to Alt-Lönnewitz, at which places it was progressively disbanded and personnel either absorbed by the *Geschwader*'s other *Gruppen* or reassigned elsewhere. Finally, IV./KG 76, led by Knight's Cross-holder Major Karl-Hermann Millahn, performed as an operational training and replacement unit based at Finow, northeast of Berlin. It remained here while awaiting delivery of Ar 234s from Arado.

Under such an infrastructure, the *Geschwaderstab*, II. and III./KG 76 commenced familiarisation on the Ar 234. It is important to stress that this was a process of 'familiarisation', rather than more thorough 'training' on the aircraft because the numbers of completed and accepted Arados at this time was minimal. However, in addition to being briefed on the assembly and technical aspects of the Ar 234 by company personnel at Alt-Lönnewitz, the *Geschwader*'s groundcrews and technical personnel were also despatched to Arado's other plants, as well as to the Zeiss works at Dresden and the BMW factory at Basdorf-Zühlsdorf, to receive instruction in instruments and (the planned) engines, respectively. In terms of the latter, with the supply of BMW units looking increasingly unlikely, Jumo 004 turbojets were delivered from Junkers at Muldenstein, southeast of Dessau, or from Magdeburg-Neustadt in Upper Silesia.

Meanwhile, as Hauptmann Lukesch organised the *Einsatzstaffel*, another Luftwaffe unit had been formed in late June at Rechlin-Lärz. The *Erprobungskommando Lärz*, known more widely as *Erprobungskommando* (*E.Kdo*) 234, was established at the Luftwaffe's *Erprobungsstelle* to assess the Ar 234 as a bomber using the short-run S-series of aircraft, or B-0s, the precursor to the main B-2 bomber series. The S-series jets would be built sequentially from Wk-Nr 140101 GM+BA as the S1 through to the S20 (Wk-Nr 140120 GM+BT), with the S1 making its first flight from Alt-Lönnewitz on 8 June 1944. *E.Kdo* 234 was placed under the command of the Austrian Oberleutnant Dr Hubert Spadiut, a highly experienced bomber pilot who is credited with having flown more than 300 missions in the Ju 88 over the USSR, North Africa, the Aegean and Italy. A recipient of the Knight's Cross, Spadiut was formerly *Kapitän* of 4./KG 76.

The intention was that all three *Gruppen* of KG 76 would have eight pilots trained by *E.Kdo* 234 as instructors. From July the *Erprobungskommando* was assigned the S1 Wk-Nr 140101 and the S5 Wk-Nr 140105 GM+BE, with which it undertook early tests, while another unidentified Ar 234 allocated to the unit was apparently the subject of a field modification incorporating a battery of machine guns on top of the fuselage behind the pilot. This is believed to have been done on the initiative of Hauptmann Dr Friedrich Harries, *Staffelkapitän* of 10.(Erg)/KG 76, another Knight's Cross-holder and expert bombing and ground-strafing pilot from the Eastern and Mediterranean fronts. Although test flights with the armament installation were considered successful, it did not meet with the approval of the RLM and no further work was undertaken.

During August nine Ar 234s assigned to KG 76 were sent to *E.Kdo* 234 at Rechlin for evaluation. Here, they also had a Patin PDS 11 three-axis autopilot, *Lotfe* bombsight for high-altitude bombing and FuG 25a IFF equipment installed. Personnel at Alt-Lönnewitz also familiarised themselves with the *Sturzkampfvisier*

Oberleutnant Dr Hubert Spadiut joined 12./KG 76 in May 1941 and flew with the *Geschwader* until December 1944. When III./KG 76 transitioned to the Ar 234, he was assigned to the *Erprobungskommando* 234 based at Rechlin, which was charged with carrying out tests on the Ar 234 with ordnance, course control systems, bombsights and other equipment (*Robert Forsyth Collection*)

5B dive-bombing sight and the *Bombenzielanlage* (BZA) targeting device used for lower level, glide-bombing attacks.

The fact that several different bombsights were trialled reflects the long-running differences of opinion between Luftwaffe pilots in respect of how best to use the Ar 234 as a bomber. In June 1944 Oberleutnant Sommer of the 1./*Versuchsverband Oberbefehlshaber der Luftwaffe* (Experimental Unit of Luftwaffe High Command) who had been assigned to fly the Ar 234 prototypes for assessment as reconnaissance aircraft, believed that the best method of bombing with the Ar 234 would be from high level. This would allow the pilot to make best use of the Arado's speed advantage over enemy fighters. Bombing accuracy could be achieved by using the *Lotfe* 7K sight, with course control aided by the PDS 11.

'Dive-bombing', Sommer wrote, 'would be necessarily inaccurate because of the high gliding speed without the braking effect of idling propellers. It would also lead the pilot into the flak danger zone and air turbulence at lower altitudes.' But this was not a view shared by the likes of Storp or Lukesch. 'It was a clash of thinking, so to speak', recalled Sommer. Indeed, Lukesch considered it 'irresponsible to order horizontal bombing without any possibility of being able to see what was happening behind us'. It was Lukesch's view that with an aircraft like the Hawker Tempest V, the Allies had the means to engage at 6000-10,000 m. Yet Sommer flew some 70 'straight-line' long-range reconnaissance missions and was never intercepted by enemy fighters as long as he retained high altitude and flew fast.

On 5 August Oberleutnant Dr Spadiut and Hauptmann Schilling of 7./KG 76 carried out what was possibly the first 'formation training flight' in a *Rotte* (two-aircraft tactical element) using Ar 234s. The aircraft's turbojets were started simultaneously, with all communication being shouted verbally on the ground. The lead jet then commenced its take-off as the *Rottenmaschine* accelerated its engines. Take-off of both Arados 'took place completely without problem, and no strong gusts from the aircraft were apparent'. After take-off, the lead aircraft flew at 350 km/h at an altitude of 500 m until it was joined by the second machine. Both aircraft then flew at 450 km/h, increasing altitude to 4000 m, at which height various manoeuvring, positioning and formation experiments were carried out – all successfully. After a short flying time at 7000 m, the lead jet had to break off due to being low on fuel, and the second Ar 234 remained in a descent behind. The 'formation' broke up over the airfield and the pilots landed without any drama.

Despite the brevity of the flight, much was learned. Importantly, from an operational perspective, the test had shown that take-offs could take place at short intervals, allow for quick formation assembly. However, because of high fuel consumption and the risk of overloading the turbojets, it became apparent that the Ar 234 could not taxi under its own power. Thus, 'for each aircraft taking-off in formation, a *Kettenkrad* [towing vehicle] must be made available. In order to avoid congestion at take-off, the turbos have to be started whilst taxiing. In this case it is necessary that the *Kettenkrad*s are equipped with an auxiliary battery for starting the turbos. The connection from the battery to the on-board connection must already be hooked-up during taxiing. In this way, under tow with a turbo in operation, the aircraft arrive quickly, one after the other, at the take-off point and can take-off immediately in short intervals.

'In normal take-offs, it has been established that the aircraft can take off very close one behind the other, since the wakes from the turbo are not very strong. A distance of 300 to 400 m after taxiing is possible. A light side wind is of advantage, since the combustion heat is thereby dispersed.'

The take-off interval would also be determined by whether the *R-Gerät* (Walter 109-500) rocket-assisted take-off (RATO) pack was used, although no practical experience with RATO had yet been gained.

There remained, however, one fundamental problem that affected formation flying, the safety of the pilot and tactical capability – the lack of rearward vision from the cockpit. Oberst Storp reported that;

'The lack of vision to the rear makes it extremely difficult to carry out a formation flight, and the sudden overshooting of an aircraft creates the very great danger of ramming. The lead aircraft in the training formation had at only one time during the entire flight seen the aircraft located behind. The leading aircraft does not have a picture of the shape and strength of the formation it is leading.'

To overcome this problem it was proposed to install a rear-view sight to the rear above and to the rear below, as well as the development of an all-round-vision periscope viewing upwards and downwards, to allow the pilot to maintain sight of aircraft flying in formation behind them, thus ensuring both his and their safety.

One of the earliest and most detailed surviving assessments of the Ar 234 was prepared by Hauptmann Josef Regler, the *Staffelkapitän* of 7./KG 76 and a former instructor with IV. *Gruppe*, on 18 July 1944. Regler was a combat-seasoned bomber pilot with more than 250 missions to his name. Having flown the S1, it was Regler's belief that the Ar 234 represented 'a new era', and that the aircraft's design, jet engines, speed and altitude capability offered enormous new tactical possibilities. He felt that because of the Arado's superior handling characteristics, most pilots should make the transition from conventional bomber aircraft with little difficulty, although he did stress the importance of sufficient instruction in the operation of the turbojet engine. He also warned that the large size of the tailplane introduced a great hazard to a pilot attempting to bail out of the aircraft, and suggested the introduction of a jettisonable door on the left of the cockpit from which a pilot could bail out and drop beneath the left wing, or to fit an ejection seat to eject upwards or downwards.

After having received a competent level of instruction on the Ar 234 from Spadiut's *Kommando*, the initial batch of pilots returned to KG 76, where they encountered a frustrating lack of aircraft during the summer of 1944 caused mainly by delays in installing the Patin PDS 11 three-axis autopilot that would be required for bombing operations. It was to be used in conjunction with the *Lotfe* 7K tachometric bombsight, temporarily

Laden with two 250 kg bombs, Ar 234 V9 PH+SQ takes off from Brandenburg, its RATO units burning to give a temporary boost in power and reducing the need for a maximum-length runway (*EN Archive*)

taking control of the aircraft in order to allow the pilot to focus on horizontal, high-level bomb-aiming.

Notwithstanding this, Hauptmann Heid pressed ahead with giving classroom instruction to his pilots and technicians in bombing methods. It was envisaged that the training of around 20 pilots and 267 technical personnel would take 24 days. Only when the training for III. *Gruppe* was completed should similar training commence for II. and IV. *Gruppen*. Despite only a small number of Ar 234s returning from Rechlin during August, III./KG 76 nevertheless managed to carry out flights for course control measurement and collimation, undercarriage trials, aircraft performance, measurement trials for Rechlin's air-dropped weapons assessment section, *Lotfe* 7K tests and three formation practice flights.

On 28 August, *E.Kdo* 234 flight-tested S2 Wk-Nr 140102 GM+BB fitted with a *Lotfe* bombsight and a Patin PDS 11 course control system that had received adjustments by Rechlin's *Abt.* E5. This exposed an overriding problem, as the *Erprobungskommando* reported;

'The trouble-free execution of a *Lotfe* target-approach flight fails with the current state of steering because of the impossibility of setting a definite altitude, and the inexact holding of the altitude. Bomb release with the *Lotfe* is dependent upon the solution of this problem.'

Finally, towards the end of the month, more Ar 234s began to trickle in to III./KG 76. The S14, Wk-Nr 140114 GM+BN, and S15, Wk-Nr 140115 GM+BO, were delivered on the 26th, while the S16, Wk-Nr 140116 GM+BP, arrived two days later. The S18, Wk-Nr 140118 GM+BR, was taken on strength on the 31st, but all these aircraft had to go to Rechlin for PDS 11 and other equipment installation.

In addition to flight training, performance charts for take-off and landing, climbing and level flight had to be prepared, as did temperature configurations and take-off weights, both with and without RATO and braking parachutes. The *Egon* radar guidance systems for blind bombing and bad weather landings with the aid of *Würzburg* radar also had to be set up and checked out. Guidelines were prepared on the new navigational systems under development, and these had to be tested and adjusted. Likewise, the *Lotfe* and BZA sights, some of which had to be re-installed based on the limited flying experience gained to that point. The pilots also carried out acceptance tests after all essential modifications had been completed.

On 5 September, Storp wrote a detailed and somewhat damning *Erfahrungsbericht* (Summary/Experience Report) in which he highlighted both the positives and shortcomings of the Ar 234. The *Geschwaderkommodore* complained that general problems persisted with the Jumo 004 turbojets, usually in the form of repeatedly occurring faults. These included failure to start due to the turbine wheel in the thrust nozzle suffering severe fire damage, cracks in a compressor and damaged Riedel starter motors. The main undercarriage lacked sufficient damping on landing and when taxiing, and this was partially solved by reducing the oil levels. There were also problems with locking the undercarriage legs down. Storp also repeated his request for steering to be incorporated into the nosewheel and for problems with the brakes to be rectified. He cited the following example;

'Through failure of the left brake, the aircraft had insufficient runway length and on its last landing rolled into a ditch, tore off its nosewheel and the cabin nosed-over into another ditch immediately behind the first. The pilot got away with a slightly bruised foot. This, however, is only thanks to the fact that on its last roll-out, the damage occurred at a speed of only 20 km/h.'

In order to reduce the danger to the pilot, Storp suggested;

1) strengthening of the underside of the cabin and installation of a glide-rail.

2) making the nosewheel traversable.

3) switching-over of the retraction sequence so that the mainwheels retracted first.

There were also deficiencies in the hydraulics system that controlled the flaps, and it was recommended that the compass, which was located in the starboard wing and caused static deviation, should be relocated to the end of the fuselage.

Of major concern was the fact that the bomb release system was not capable of carrying and releasing three 'large-calibre' bombs, with the switching/timing/sequencing system offering just two options. According to Storp;

'At a speed of 700 km/h this gives a separation of 13.6 m and 65 m from bomb to bomb. These two setting possibilities are not sufficient for the effectiveness of large-calibre bombs. According to the type and effective radius of the bombs, a variable separation setting must be available. In order that the bombs dropped in sequence attain their full effectiveness, a setting possibility of the sequence separation from 20 m to 300 m and infinitely variable, or in 20 m separations, is required.'

Internally the airspeed indicator was deemed insufficient for navigation. Adjustment was also required for the BZA sighting periscope since pilots had found that from the normal seated position in the cockpit they were not able to see through the ocular, which was too high. Storp reported;

'In order to see through the ocular in the current installation the pilot has to be seated so high that with the periscope sight, due to the flat angle in the upper portion of the Plexiglas canopy and the thick frame of the canopy, the field of vision is hindered. In flight at over 750 km/h, vibrations in the BZA periscope occurred that caused the target image to disappear completely. These vibrations in the optical field of vision are probably caused by the aerodynamically insufficient cockpit frames and the unstable installation of the projecting part of the periscope.'

Importantly, also in August, because some – at least four – Arados had reached III./KG 76, *Oberkommando der Luftwaffe* (OKL) was of the view that the *Gruppe* was sufficiently ready to relocate to Burg-bei-Magdeburg airfield, 150 km to the northwest of Alt-Lönnewitz, from where it could prepare for offensive operations in the west. To this end, on the 29th, as Hauptmann

Walter Storp, seen here as a Major, shortly after being decorated with the Oak Leaves to the Knight's Cross in July 1941. Originally a maritime aviator in the mid-1930s, during which period he served as a pilot on board the pocket battleship *Admiral Scheer*, he had flown combat missions over Dunkirk, the Soviet Union and Italy by war's end. Storp commanded KG 76 between June and October 1944, overseeing the *Geschwader's* transition from the Ju 88 to the Ar 234 (*EN Archive*)

Regler and Hauptmann Neumann of the *Gruppe's* servicing company oversaw the logistics for moving the bulk of the *Gruppe*, Hauptmann Lukesch departed Alt-Lönnewitz with a *Vorkommando* comprising two men from each *Staffel*, a two-man signals section and three personnel from the unit's servicing company. Bound for Burg, Lukesch and his men arrived there on 1 September to prepare accommodation and assess the surrounding area. However, with so few aircraft available, the *Vorkommando's* technical specialists were assigned to the appropriate Arado manufacturing plants as an interim measure in order to obtain more experience on the Ar 234.

Gradually, III./KG 76 settled in at its new base, and to counter any sense of treading water, Storp (who was still at Alt-Lönnewitz) made all efforts to ensure that his personnel at Burg kept active mentally and physically in preparation for impending operations. His attitude was summarised by a succinct line in a report of 7 September in which he set out in detail what he saw as a standard set of training guidelines for the 'Conversion of a *Kampfgruppe* onto the Ar 234. New aircraft – new methods – new tactics!'

Storp had concluded that it would take eight weeks to fully instruct flying and technical personnel through a combination of practical lessons and classroom tuition. In addition, following an initial six training flights in an Ar 234 for pilots, it would be necessary to carry out two target practice flights and three bomb-dropping practice flights in a He 111 – the venerable twin-engined bomber was the aircraft in which it was felt the most appropriate training could be given. Once this had been done, a further three training flights in an Ar 234 would be needed.

The flying programme was bolstered with the arrival of eight more Ar 234s between 5 and 23 September – Wk-Nr 140119 (S19) GM+BS was delivered first on the 5th, but it was initially forced to remain grounded pending a delivery of J2 fuel. It was followed by Wk-Nr 140117 (S17) GM+BQ (subsequently sent to 7./KG 76 as F1+DR), Wk-Nr 140120 (S20) GM+BT (subsequently sent to 8./KG 76 as F1+QS), Wk-Nr 140143 SM+FC, Wk-Nr 140141 SM+FA, Wk-Nr 140144 SM+FD, Wk-Nr 140146 SM+FF (subsequently F1+CS) and Wk-Nr 140147 SM+FG.

However, while aircraft may have started to arrive, they were being delivered with problems, as Oberleutnant Dr Spadiut noted;

'The frequent occurrence of ground faults and short-circuits due to the effects of moisture is almost intolerable, and this would especially be the case with aircraft parked out in the open at a frontline operational airfield. Faults occurred not only in the rain, but also in the high air humidity. The fastest possible elimination of this situation is vital, since otherwise an aircraft equipped with such high-quality and sensitive electrical equipment will have only a very slight chance of being flight-cleared. The same has been observed by the *E-Stelle* Rechlin.'

There was also still a problem with supplies of the bombing equipment needed to conduct operations. On 2 September, Oberleutnant Spitzer, an officer from KG 76 assigned to E.Kdo 234, visited the Zeiss Ikon works in Dresden to investigate likely delivery of the badly needed BZA 1b bombsight for dive- and glide-bombing operations. Spitzer was assured that the sights would arrive within two or three days, but this assurance proved hollow. The crux of the matter was that Spitzer was concerned over the performance of the BZA with the already reported vibration of the cockpit PV 1b periscope encountered at speeds of 700 km/h and higher. This was attributable to poor mounting of the periscope and lack of cooperation between its Munich-based manufacturer and Arado. Spitzer stressed in his report of 11 September;

'Removal of this deficiency is vital. Bomb release with the BZA and a periscope will meet with problems, for on the one hand the pilot has to lean forward to the right in order to be able to see at all, whereby he loses the feel for the correct position of the aircraft, and on the other hand, during diving flight, it is not possible for him to simultaneously observe the instruments, as was the case with the *Stuvi* 5B [dive-bombing sight].'

A few days later Spitzer called on the help of the *Kommandeur* of the *Erprobungsstelle* Rechlin, Oberstleutnant Edmund Daser, to secure a vehicle and communication equipment to assist in BZA training. There were still no bombsights, however.

At Burg, Hauptmann Heid reported on the poor standard of construction of the small number of Ar 234s there. Just about all aspects were affected – engines, airframes, radio equipment and bomb-release mechanisms. The *Gruppenkommandeur* was particularly aggrieved to discover in one incident that a pencil had been found jammed in the rudder steering mechanism of an aircraft – the result, possibly, of sabotage or shoddy workmanship.

This frustrating situation was compounded by other technical problems associated with the *Lotfe* 7K sight intended for horizontal bombing that prevented any ordnance from being dropped over the waters of the Müritzsee at Rechlin by mid-September. Dropping trials were hastily rearranged, with Ar 234 S15 Wk-Nr 140115 expending bombs on a field near Rechlin. The jet was fitted with a robot camera to record flight and release data, although sighting this equipment proved challenging for the pilot as its position resulted in a loss of vision from the cockpit. The possibility of using a swivel arm for the camera was negated by the vibrations of the PV 1b periscope.

A specialist bombing instructor from II./KG 101 had been called in to provide tuition to the pilots, and he was expected to arrive at Rechlin in a few days. Notwithstanding this, Spitzer was of the opinion that the *Lotfe* sight was too cumbersome and prone to faults. Diether Lukesch, who was not an advocate for high-level bombing with the Ar 234, supported this view, recalling that the *Lotfe*/PDS combination did not function reliably and that training flights were frequently hampered by enemy fighter incursions or by fog. In any case, a prospective *Lotfe* training course to be conducted over the Galenbecker See devised by II./KG 101 was postponed because aircraft could not be spared.

By the end of September, III./KG 76 had seen its Arados take off on 21 occasions, representing a total flying time of 8 hours 54 mins. Twenty-two more Ar 234s arrived in October, but faults and poor build quality persisted. Prior to being ferried to Burg, aircraft were re-doped at Alt-Lönnewitz without first being cleaned. With the application of colour paint on dust and dirt, rough external surfaces resulted and airworthiness was adversely affected. There were damaged ball bearings found in the rudder trimming mechanism and components were missing from Riedel starter motors. As it arrived at Burg from Alt-Lönnewitz, smoke streamed from the brakes of Wk-Nr 140156 SM+FP, while brake and rudder problems plagued

In November 1944, Oberstleutnant Robert Kowalewski was appointed as *Kommodore* of KG 76. A highly experienced and capable commander, he flew 280 bomber missions over the Western and Mediterranean fronts and was credited with the sinking of 16 merchant ships (*Robert Forsyth Collection*)

Wk-Nr 140158 SM+FR and Wk-Nr 140163 BM+LC. On 12 October, Leutnant Hans-Egon Arndt of 8./KG 76 suffered injuries when he attempted to take off from Rechlin in the S16, Wk-Nr seen 140116 F1+BS, and he died the next day.

For all the challenges and adversities facing KG 76 in its battle to bring the Ar 234 fully up to operational status, the deteriorating war situation for Germany meant that the jet bomber's operational debut could not come soon enough. By late October, troops of Field Marshal Bernard Montgomery's 21st Army Group had reached the southern banks of the Scheldt River and American forces had taken Aachen, in Germany.

That same month Oberst Storp was appointed *General der Kampfflieger*, and in a sign that operations by KG 76 were imminent, his successor was quickly named as Oberstleutnant Robert Kowalewski, a very accomplished bomber and anti-shipping pilot and holder of the Knight's Cross since November 1940. He had seen combat in operations over England, the Mediterranean as *Kommandeur* of II./KG 26, the Bay of Biscay and the Atlantic as *Kommandeur* of III./KG 40 and, more recently, as *Kommodore* of the Bf 110- and Me 410-equipped ZG 76 in the *Reichsverteidigung* (Defence of the Reich).

Thirty-four Ar 234s were assigned to III./KG 76 in November, with 12 being relayed to *E.Kdo* 234 for testing and installation of equipment during the same month. Although casualties were minimal, on 10 November Unteroffizier Karl Fritschet of 9./KG 76 was killed as a result of a technical fault during an *Egon* training flight from Burg in Wk-Nr 140170 F1+GS – he attempted to bail out but he was too low for his parachute to open. Unteroffizier Ludwig Rieffel from the same *Staffel* was able to escape with light injuries when Wk-Nr 140327 crashed to the east of Burg following engine failure on the 19th.

At the end of November Kowalewski noted, 'Promising operational use with the current aircraft is not expected.' But this held little sway with *Reichsmarschall* Göring, who was demanding that KG 76 be ready as soon as possible to commence operations over the Western Front. He wanted each Ar 234 to carry at least one 500 kg bomb, but there was still dissent between the *Geschwader*, the *Erprobungsstelle* at Rechlin, the office of the *General der Kampfflieger* and the OKL as to how best to deploy the Arados in terms of high-level, horizontal bombing with the *Lotfe* 7K sight or in low-level, glide- or gentle dive-bombing attacks with the BZA sight.

Thus it was that on 16 November 1944, III./KG 76 officially formed an *Einsatzstaffel* (Operations Squadron) drawn mainly from personnel of 9./KG 76 with a strength of between ten and twelve Ar 234s to be led by the *Staffelkapitän* of 9. *Staffel*, Hauptmann Lukesch. In fact, a *Vorkommando* had already departed Burg on the 10th for the *Einsatzstaffel*'s new base at Münster-Handorf, while in a sign of the pressure applied by Göring, every Ar 234 that did not require 'accelerated re-arming for operational purposes' was assigned to the new *Staffel*. The time was approaching for the world's first jet-bomber to make its combat debut.

CHAPTER TWO

RECONNAISSANCE – 1944

esting of the Ar 234 in the reconnaissance role had been underway at Rechlin since April 1944, with Hauptmann Horst Götz and Oberleutnant Erich Sommer of the *Versuchsverband* OKL joining the programme in June to explore high-altitude endurance. Orders for Ar 234 operations in the West went out from *Luftflotte* 3 on 24 July – Cherbourg, seen as critical to the fighting in Normandy, would be the main target, with coverage of the English mainland coming later. Like other reconnaissance units on the invasion front, the two-jet detachment would operate under the control of *Fernaufklärungsgruppe* (FAGr.) 123.

On 25 July Sommer brought Ar 234 V7 Wk-Nr 130007 T9+MH to Juvincourt, about 20 km northwest of Reims, with supporting ground equipment arriving aboard a Ju 352 transport. History's first jet reconnaissance operation was to have followed on 1 August but, as was so often the case in the Ar 234's career, bad weather intervened. Improved conditions the next day saw Sommer in the air from 1332 to 1525 hrs photographing the invasion area. British intelligence learned of this from a despatch sent by a Japanese diplomat, who managed to confuse the Me 262, Me 163 and Ar 234;

'Me 262 rocket fighters used on recent daylight Leipzig raid not a success because only three used and time they can stay up, but those used for daylight photo-recce over invasion beaches North France on 2nd August were most successful.'

Oberleutnant Erich Sommer brought the skid-equipped Ar 234 V7 (Wk-Nr 130007 T9+MH) to Juvincourt on 25 July 1944. A take-off accident on 1 November ended its operational career (*EN Archive*)

The view from the cockpit on 2 August 1944 as Oberleutnant Sommer flies history's first jet reconnaissance sortie, securing copious intelligence on Allied unloading operations in the Normandy bridgehead (*EN Archive*)

Ju 352 T9+AB of the *Vesuchsverband* OKL ferried equipment to Juvincourt to support the first Ar 234 operations. At right is Oberleutnant Erich Sommer (*EN Archive*)

The detachment's other pilot, Hauptmann Horst Götz, had flown Ar 234 V5 Wk-Nr 130005 T9+LH to Juvincourt from Oranienburg shortly before Sommer's return, but with only one RATO set on hand, further sorties had to await new deliveries. Sommer was told it took 24 man-days to interpret the yield from his first sortie, with this detailed evaluation discussed by the *Kriegsmarine* on 4 August showing why;

'Bernières northwest of the Orne Mouth: 200,000 GRT, 2 cruisers, 8 MTB, 34 escort and minesweepers, 245 LCT and small landing craft.

'North of Asnelles: 130,000 GRT, 48 MTB, 38 escort and minesweepers, 5 LSTs, 115 LCT and small landing craft.

'North of Laurence: probably old battleship as breakwater, 490,000 GRT, 1 MTB, 7 LST/LCI, 122 LCT and small boats.

'Northwest of the Vire mouth: 360,000 GRT, 15 minesweepers, 189 LCT and small landing craft. Smaller unloading points NW of the Orne mouth with a breakwater for the use of small vessels made from the beached *Courbet*; 1 *Java* [-class cruiser], 1 destroyer and 6 freighters of 42,000 GRT aground.

'North of Luc: 21.000 GRT, 18 MTB, 81 LCT and small landing craft.

'Breakwaters constructed from merchantmen off the main points: at Bernières with 77,000 GRT; at Asnelles with 296,000 GRT, 72 caissons, 5 landing stages and 2 floating docks; at Laurence with 56,000 GRT and 45 caissons; at the Vire mouth out of 64,000 GRT with 2 landing-stages.

'Total occupancy of the Seine Bay consisted of: 2 cruisers, 2 destroyers, 45 escorts, 74 MTB, 43 minesweepers, 1 landing transport, 13 LST, 278 LCI, 520 smaller landing craft, 5 transports (26,000 GRT), 180 freighters (1,157,000 GRT), 6 tankers (20,500 GRT), 2 old battleships, 1 old cruiser

Hauptmann Horst Götz's Ar 234 V5 Wk-Nr 130005 T9+LH crash-landed at Oranienburg after damage from friendly flak. An Fw 190 then collided with it, completing the Arado's destruction (*EN Archive*)

and 50 freighters (335,000 GRT) used as breakwaters. Number of cruisers, destroyers and tankers is strikingly low.'

The films themselves were processed by technicians of 1.(F)/121 and 1./NAG 13, and photographs survive from the inaugural flight, plus another by Sommer on the 4th and one by Götz on 12 August (these last two missions covered Cherbourg, with results noted by the *Kriegsmarine*). The two Arados remained at Juvincourt until the Allied breakout forced the detachment's withdrawal to Chièvres, in Belgium, on 28 August. Götz suffered a mishap en route, Sommer reporting five days later 'all that is known is T9+LH was forced to make a crash landing as a result of a direct hit from flak. The landing was made in Oranienburg. After landing, it was completely destroyed by a Fw 190 that was taking off.' For the next month the *Kommando* apparently consisted of just one aircraft.

British intelligence first heard the name of *Kommando Sperling* (Detachment Sparrow) following the Ar 234 unit's hasty move to Volkel, in Holland, on 30 August. On 3 September that airfield was bombed, pushing the detachment back across the German border to Rheine. Operations had resumed by the 11th, when ports and airfields in eastern England were covered, while the following day brought photo-reconnaissance of bridges over Belgium's Albert Canal, as well as Lowestoft, Great Yarmouth and the Thames Estuary. *Luftflotte* 3's orders for FAGr. 123 on the 13th were to cover advances from the 21st Army Group's bridgehead over the Meuse–Escaut (Maas–Scheldt) Canal at Beringen, as well as airfields around the Wash, especially any occupied by gliders. It seems then that even before the commencement of Operation *Market Garden* on 17 September, the Germans feared an airborne assault.

On the second day of the offensive, the *Luftflotte* ordered reconnaissance extended to the Thames Estuary, Harwich and Great Yarmouth. *Kommando Sperling* was to ready its aircraft immediately, with 'emergency measures' being taken to restore Rheine's operability after Allied bombing. By 21 September the detachment was being ordered to cover airfields in the region bounded by St Quentin, Paris and Reims, and it would return there the following day. Its orders partially read as follows;

'The main thing is to establish how far the enemy air force has moved forward in France. Bridges at Beringen are to be flown over and are to be covered by P/R [photo-reconnaissance] in order to establish position and effects of hits in the last composite aircraft operation [on 14 September, 1./KG 101 had been ordered to attack the bridge "with all available composite aircraft" – *Misteln*].'

On 23 September Ar 234B-2 Wk-Nr 140112 was delivered to the *Versuchsverband* OKL as T9+GH, and it would become Hauptmann Götz's regular machine. The B-series represented a major advance over the V5 and V7, using conventional landing gear rather than a take-off trolley.

On the 26th, *Kommando Sperling* was once again assigned the Paris–Reims area and the Beringen bridges, and the following day it was instructed to establish if trains were running again in the liberated areas. The morning of 28 September saw Sommer photographing his former base at Juvincourt, while Götz asked FAGr. 123 to collect a film containing photographs of the Paris–Reims–St Quentin area and the Albert Canal. The unit's orders for the 29th were to photograph harbours in the Thames Estuary and England's east coast as far north as Great Yarmouth, plus airfields up to the Wash.

Three days later, Götz flew T9+GH on a photo-reconnaissance mission over Antwerp, Turnhout, Grave and Nijmegen, with Sommer (T9+MH) also covering these areas, plus Saint Trond (Sint Truiden) and Maastricht. On the 4th Götz was asked whether Cherbourg and Le Havre could be reached with auxiliary tanks or from a forward base. British intelligence noted that the last reconnaissance mission over the Seine Bay that could be definitely identified had taken place on 15 August, and that recently 'only one report of Detachment GOETZ has been received, with "all the old airfields" reported to have been photographed'.

T9+GH (Wk-Nr 140112) joined *Kommando Sperling* on 23 September 1944, after which it was the regular aircraft of the *Kommandoführer*, Hauptmann Horst Götz, until his detachment's operational responsibilities were handed over to 1.(F)/123 in February 1945. He would return to lead that *Staffel* following the death of its *Kapitän*, Hauptmann Hans Felde, on 11 February 1945 (*EN Archive*)

Sommer was in Berlin on 4 October, but orders to reconnoitre 'the remainder of southeast England' were given for the following two days (and would keep being given). On the 6th the *Kommando* was asked for 'results of flights with auxiliary tank with approximate range Le Havre', and that afternoon Götz was requesting that film be collected immediately. Flying T9+GH, he had undertaken a successful reconnaissance of southeast England, seeing 'no important shipping traffic', but by evening his aircraft was unserviceable. Coverage of England the following morning was thwarted by cloud up to 10,000 m, so Limburg was photographed instead on the way home. Allied fighters were seen but had not tried to intercept. Returning to the coast, the Arado's unnamed pilot saw 'one shot from rocket *Flak* or special weapon' passing 100 m from his aircraft and rising almost vertically to about 11,000 m. Götz had recently requested the location of V2 batteries and was told they were launching from the Rotterdam–Den Haag area.

Orders for the 8th included photographing Allied penetrations south of Geilenkirchen – the *Kommando* was urged to secure coverage 'under all circumstances' and advised that the morning's weather forecast militated against flights to England. Over the following four days the unit was

T9+HH (Wk-Nr 140153) joined *Kommando Sperling* on 11 October 1944, the aircraft usually being flown by Leutnant Wolfgang Ziese. Six days after its assignment to the detachment the jet was used to secure photographs of Antwerp and Ostend (*EN Archive*)

Taking off with RATO assistance, T9+KH (Wk-Nr 140151) joined *Kommando Sperling* at Rheine in late October 1944. Its regular pilot was Oberleutnant Werner Muffey (*EN Archive*)

Muffey's T9+KH featured a cartoon of a 'jet-propelled' sparrow (*Sperling* in German) beneath the cockpit glazing (*EN Archive*)

Pairs of RATO packs assisted the Ar 234's take-off, especially when carrying extra weight such as drop tanks or bombs. In January 1945, the Rechlin Trials Establishment raised concerns that cold weather might affect combustion and cause swerving during the take-off run (*EN Archive*)

tasked with photographing Walcheren (where the Battle of the Scheldt had recently opened), southeast England and Le Havre.

A third Ar 234 (Wk-Nr 140153 T9+HH) joined *Sperling* on 11 October, its regular pilot being Leutnant Wolfgang Ziese. Two days later the OKL belatedly notified the General of Flak Training of the Ar 234's identifying features, explaining that 'jet units are engines without propellers'. Orders to cover Ostend and Antwerp were fulfilled by T9+HH that afternoon.

By 17 October the *Kommando* had been reinforced by Wk-Nr 140454 and 140154 (T9+IH), the latter becoming Sommer's machine. The *Kommando*'s targets for 20 October were 'P/R's road bridge Nijmegen, Walcheren, Antwerp and bridgehead Breskens, completion of P/R SE England'. Pictures of Antwerp were perhaps required for a planned *Mistel* and bombing attack on the Van Cauwelaert Lock at Kruisschans, linking the River Scheldt to the harbour. In mid-September, swimming saboteurs had left the gates 'considerably battered', but KG 66 was advised on 26 October that 'degree of damage achieved is too slight and usability only slightly impaired (according to P/R)'. Oberleutnant Werner Muffey (see below) recalled flying reconnaissance for V2 launches against this target, seeing 'a double lift-off on the horizon but after the calculated three minutes had elapsed, no detonation near the lock. Finally, a spot on my film turned out to be the crater, which I had taken to be steam from a locomotive, 12 km off target.'

On the afternoon of the 21st, Sommer (T9+IH) photographed Walcheren, Zeebrugge, Ostend and Antwerp. Most of Walcheren was flooded, and there were three fires in the Breskens pocket (a German enclave south of the Scheldt, then coming under attack). Unusual orders were issued on the 22nd, apparently to photograph Army Group B's HQ at Osterath. Three days

A pair of expended RATO packs descending on their recovery parachutes, which were fitted at the front so that the *R-Gerät* could be reused after being dropped from the Ar 234. The rockets burned for 30 seconds before being jettisoned (*EN Archive*)

later, the Chief of Staff to *Oberbefehlshaber West* (Supreme Commander West) told Army Groups B and G that 'Strategic air recce, even though on a small scale, is assured by some Ar 234s of *Kommando Götz* [as *Sperling* was still sometimes referred to], which, for the present, is to receive the recce a/c coming from the factories.'

On 27 October, a directive went out that code words including *Zinn* and *Orkan* ('tin' and 'hurricane' for the Ar 234 and Jumo 004, respectively) must be used in teleprinter and telephone traffic. Sometime between 23 and 29 October, Wk-Nr 140151 (T9+KH) joined the *Kommando*. It was flown by Oberleutnant Muffey, who would become the unit's Technical Officer;

'Major [Wolfgang] Heese [the *Versuchsverband*'s Deputy CO] disclosed to me very confidentially that I had immediately to join *Kommando Götz* [and] tomorrow, should be sufficient to make myself familiar with the Ar 234. [I had] never before experienced hair-raising speed [but] made a marvellously smooth landing. Full of praise for the amiable behaviour of my new kite, I lost all inhibition and wanted to go as soon as possible over to Rheine.'

Meanwhile, T9+GH had become unserviceable, seemingly through engine trouble. On the 30th, Ziese (T9+HH) and Sommer (T9+IH) flew morning missions. The next day T9+MH was finally reported serviceable, but while taking off on an operation on 1 November one of its skids collapsed. Although Feldwebel Walter Wendt escaped uninjured, the aircraft's rudder and fuselage were damaged and it was returned to Oranienburg for repair but was struck off four weeks later. Ultra intercepts by British intelligence disclosed that a *Sperling* Arado was forced to break off from its mission because of bad weather, corresponding with the *Versuchsverband*'s report that Muffey (T9+KH) operated from 1332 to 1428 hrs on 1 November.

The following day, Sommer carried out an order from *Luftwaffenkommando West* (*Lw.Kdo. West* – Air Command West) to take off immediately for Vlissingen, checking on the weather and the whereabouts of shipping, possibly in connection with proposed midget submarine and explosive motorboat operations in the Scheldt. On the 3rd, despite Rheine reporting that it was 'unserviceable' due to poor weather, Muffey nevertheless took off from there for an 18-minute flight, before turning back when encountering thickening cloud. The attempt to fly this mission in such conditions reflected the fact that the reconnaissance programme was well behind schedule. Indeed, on both 2 and 3 November orders were issued for road and rail cover 'in accordance with [Order] No 14979 of 19 October'.

On 4 November Ziese (T9+HH) flew a 90-minute morning operation taking in railways, roads and bridges in Belgium and southern Holland, along with photography of Vlissingen, Ghent, Antwerp, Breda, Tilburg and 's-Hertogenbosch. Muffey took up T9+KH at midday for photo-reconnaissance of the frontline, returning after his starboard engine failed. This grounded the aircraft for six days. On the 5th the *Kommando* was again ordered to cover the Kruisschans lock ('if possible at ebb tide'), plus roads, railways and bridges. Poor weather meant that no flights took place, however. Wendt (T9+GH) flew on the 6th, as did Sommer (T9+IH), while Götz got airborne in T9+GH on the 7th, only to again turn back because of inclement weather.

For 8 November the targets were to be Allied airfields in Belgium and Holland, while continuous railway cover was to be undertaken as soon as the weather would permit. That same day, Sommer was arranging for Biblis, near Worms, to be stocked with RATO packs. The 10th brought orders alerting Biblis to T9+IH's imminent arrival. The Operations Officer (Flying) of *Lw.Kdo. West* ordered *Sperling* to send one and if possible two Ar 234s there that day, provided one serviceable machine remained in Rheine. With only T9+HH and T9+IH having been operational for the previous 72 hours, just a single aircraft was detached. This new emphasis on photo-reconnaissance coverage of the southern part of the frontline may have been a reaction to the deteriorating German position in the battle for Metz, and the distinct possibility of a US Army breakthrough to the *Reich* border. Nevertheless, Dutch and Belgian airfields were covered on the afternoon of the 10th.

The following day *Lw.Kdo. West* passed urgent orders to *Sperling* for '1) road and railway reconnaissance, area Brussels–Sedan–Liège, and 2) airfields on both sides of line Nijmegen–Eindhoven and Liège–Louvain'. Muffey flew the second of these assignments, although his T9+KH was unserviceable by evening. The next day *Lw.Kdo. West* asked *Sperling* if it had arrangements for passing orders to *Kommando Hecht* (Pike). It is not known why this name was chosen, Bletchley Park mistakenly surmising that, 'Hecht is a man who commands part of Det. Sperling'.

Götz was ordered to report to *Lw.Kdo. West* on 15 November, and the next known operation was on the 18th when *Hecht*'s lone Arado covered a range of Belgian targets, plus Sedan and Metz. Two airfields were seen under construction north of Metz and

Pilots from *Kommando Sperling*. They are, from left to right, Leutnant Wolfgang Ziese, Feldwebel Walter Wendt, Hauptmann Horst Götz, Oberleutnant zur See Böhmer (*Kriegsmarine* naval liaison officer) and Oberleutnant Werner Muffey (*EN Archive*)

one of them was photographed, as was a new one northwest of St Trond. Back at Oranienburg, Feldwebel Wendt was killed in a take-off accident on the 19th. Two sorties were flown over Holland from Rheine that same day, while *Kommando Hecht* completed a morning sortie photographing Trier, Luxembourg, Longwy, Étain and Verdun. *Sperling* achieved only partial success with coverage of Eindhoven and Nijmegen.

On 24 November Sommer took off from Rheine in T9+IH and landed at Biblis 50 minutes later. Grounded by weather yet again the following day, *Sperling* could not fulfil an order to reconnoitre an Allied artillery deployment identified northwest of Roermond by direction-finding. Both *Kommando*s flew on the 26th, however, over Holland, Belgium, Luxembourg and eastern France. Despite both T9+GH and T9+KH having engine trouble, photographs were taken and Sommer's imagery was couriered to *Lw.Kdo. West* by a *Storch*.

In the early hours of 29 November *Lw.Kdo. West* issued the following orders;

'A) Previous recce orders are invalid and are to be destroyed.

'B) Instructions on recce tasks which have been issued orally remain essentially in force.

'C) Orders for 29/11. Recce of Maas crossings from Liège to Givet. In case this cannot be carried out at high level because of the weather, recce is to be forced through at lower level. Send films from flights without delay.

'D) Alternative objectives for *Sperling* and *Hecht*: airfields in the area of Brussels–Charleroi–Liège–Hasselt, south bank of Waal from Tiel to Estuary – and roads Besançon–Belfort–Mulhouse.'

At the same time, FAGr. 123 and its subordinated units were placed under II. *Jagdkorps* control, leaving just the Ar 234s directly controlled by *Lw.Kdo. West*. These developments foreshadowed the impending German offensive in the West, implementing a plan set out on 14 November;

'Thorough P/R of attack zone before attack, as far as the rear of artillery zone, and of Meuse crossings.'

Orders for the first three days of December included looking for tanks and ammunition dumps near Nijmegen. Once the weather lifted, covering the Meuse crossings between Liège and Givet was of 'the greatest urgency'. Alternatives for *Sperling* were Antwerp and the Scheldt Estuary, while *Hecht* covered roads between Mulhouse, Belfort and Basle. On the morning of the 3rd, Ziese took T9+GH over the Scheldt and Nijmegen, and T9+KH obtained photographs of the Meuse crossings.

Four days later, a report based on Ultra intercepts deciphered at Bletchley Park noted 'The only operation of interest is the demand for coverage of unloading facilities at Antwerp sent to Det. *Sperling*. This follows a general request from the German Navy for more comprehensive recce of the Scheldt now that the port of Antwerp is functioning again'. Nevertheless, the next Operational Watch report from signals intercepts noted how coverage of the Meuse crossings 'remained first call on Ar 234 detachments'.

Further operations were impossible until the afternoon of the 12th, and the next day *Hecht's* T9+IH was at Rheine having its engines changed. Mist in the Meuse Valley thwarted coverage on the 14th, although both Liège and Namur – on the planned German lines of advance – were photographed and a *Storch* carried the films to the high command. Three sorties were mounted

Oberleutnant Erich Sommer flew the first ever jet reconnaissance operation, on 2 August 1944. He went on to lead *Kommando Hecht* at Biblis and *Kommando Sommer* in Italy (*EN Archive*)

on 16 December, the opening day of the Ardennes offensive. T9+IH's new engines gave trouble, but Ziese and Muffey successfully covered the Liège–Huy–Namur–Dinant area. All four *Sperling* and *Hecht* machines and their pilots were declared ready on the 18th, and Sommer combined his return to Biblis with a visual report including a 'very considerable number of vehicles' heading for Malmedy. A single flight the next day established that road bridges at Namur, Givet and Dinant remained in use. Götz flew on the 23rd, although he encountered visibility so bad that he was unsure exactly where he had been – he also reported a heavy Allied fighter presence.

At 1245 hrs on Christmas Eve, Erich Sommer took off from Biblis but could not return after it was bombed. Low on fuel and finding three alternates similarly damaged, he approached Wiesbaden-Erbenheim, only for T9+IH to be set on fire by that airfield's flak. Nevertheless, he was able to pull off an emergency landing, emerge unhurt and save his film magazines. *Sperling* signalled to ask whether his aircraft was repairable, to which Sommer responded that the forward fuel tank and centre section were burnt out – the Ar 234 would have to be sent to a workshop. Asked what specialists and equipment were needed to strip his damaged aeroplane, he requested that a lorry be sent next morning. Meanwhile, at Rheine, T9+GH was having its port engine changed.

With the German offensive stalled, it was decided on Christmas Day that all Ar 234 reconnaissance flights should start from Rheine for the time being and, once reinforcements had arrived, *Sperling* should hold a pilot at readiness for V2 spotting over Antwerp 'in accordance with oral instructions to Hauptmann Götz'. The 25th also saw cloudless skies for once, and Muffey and Ziese took off in quick succession to cover the battle area, Nijmegen and Tilburg. Erich Sommer, meanwhile, was travelling by car to *Lw.Kdo. West*'s photographic section. On the 26th, Muffey fulfilled a task assigned a week earlier – photographing the English coast from Southwold to Dover then Boulogne, Calais, Dunkirk, Ostend, Zeebrugge, the Scheldt and Antwerp. He later recalled such a flight;

'Crossing the coastline near Lowestoft at around 10,000 m and in a clear blue sky, trailing long white condensed streams for everyone to see. I can't remember just how many airfields we counted on the film I had brought back, full of Fortresses and Liberators, but that had been the order – to start early enough [so as] to still have them on the film before they had left their base, heading for Germany.'

Ziese was also up on the 25th, monitoring V2 impacts on Antwerp. He reported the first at 1307 hrs 7.5 km south-southwest of the city centre, west of the Willebroek road, the second four minutes later in the angle of 'the Turnhout–Meuse canal' (probably the junction of the Kempisch and Albert Canals), and the third rocket at 1314 hrs, at Rijkevorsel, 30 km east-northeast of the city. Photographs were taken of the impact points and of the Scheldt as far as Vlissingen, as well as of Antwerp itself, Breda, Tilburg, 's-Hertogenbosch and Nijmegen.

An overhead view of the cameras installed in the rear fuselage of an Ar 234, this photograph showing how they were offset from the vertical to give coverage of a wider strip of ground (*EN Archive*)

Götz (T9+HH) was in the air from 0853 hrs on the 27th for photography over Holland and Belgium, reporting cloudless skies but 'medium haze from Antwerp'. Muffey (T9+KH) took off a few minutes later, covering targets including Bastogne (where the siege had just been broken) and the Meuse bridges between Vise and Liège, finding the whole area cloudless but subject to heavy haze. An extensive interpretation report was compiled despite the Arado's starboard camera jamming after just 50 exposures, while the other's shots were fogged every three-and-a-half frames. Four days later, these results were still being cited as the latest reconnaissance of Bastogne.

A signal of 28 December described *Hecht's* status following the bombing of Biblis on Christmas Eve. Take-off and landing would be possible that day with an 1100 m strip marked out, and this would be extended to 1300 m over the next few days. The *Gefechtsstand* (Battle HQ) needed rebuilding, and some difficulty was foreseen in establishing the necessary signal lines. The sole fatality from the raid (Unteroffizier Knauf) had been buried, and the condition of the remaining wounded in hospital at Bensheim was satisfactory.

Sommer told Biblis on the 29th that an Ar 234 had arrived 'here' for *Kommando Hecht*, and that he would fly it over after a 'small conversion'. Both T9+EH (Wk-Nr 140344) and T9+LH had been delivered to Rheine and were undergoing inspection, the former machine being destined for *Hecht*. Significantly for jet reconnaissance over southern Germany, elements of 1.(F)/100's photographic platoon had reached Biblis (the *Staffel* had been on the Eastern Front until September, and it received the first of three Ar 234s at Jüterbog-Waldlager during December).

On the morning of the 29th, Ziese was airborne on weather reconnaissance for just 19 minutes. The following day *Jagdgeschwader* (JG) 6's Operations Officer warned that 'several attacks by our own fighters on Ar 234, particularly when the aircraft type in question is landing, give occasion once again for reference to the employment of this new aircraft model. Thorough instruction of all pilots in this matter must be carried out.' Nothing further is known of such attacks, even though almost all of the reconnaissance Arados' daily reports are available from this period.

On the morning of 31 December, *Sperling* was advised that Sommer was to take off at 0930 hrs under the call sign *Vagabund* (vagabond). Muffey (T9+KH) photographed Antwerp, Tirlemont (Tienen), St Trond, Roermond and Venlo, with a courier collecting his films. Rheine was strafed by fighters but no damage was done, and new aircraft T9+AH was ferried to *Sperling*. After the customary inspection, it was declared operational on 3 January.

Changing a film magazine on T9+GH. Access to the cameras was achieved by removing two rectangular hatches atop the fuselage. The Ar 234 was low enough to the ground to allow technicians access to the cameras without the need for ladders (*EN Archive*)

CHAPTER THREE

BOMBER DEBUT

Luftwaffe officers and a man, second from left, who appears to be a civilian pilot, possibly from Arado, watch an Ar 234 of KG 76 being refuelled with J2 through its forward filler point from an Opel Blitz bowser at Alt-Lönnewitz. Note the technician at right is about to use the drop-down step and handhold to climb atop the fuselage (*EN Archive*)

Possibly the earliest appearance of the *Einsatzstaffel*/KG 76 in tactical documents is in a directive of 14 November 1944 when the new unit is shown as part of the Order of Battle for the 3.*Fliegerdivision* based at Bad Essen under Generalmajor Sigismund *Freiherr* von Falkenstein. It shared its assignment with the Me 262 bombers of I./KG 51, and both units were given the task – officially at least – of providing air support for *Heeresgruppen* B and H on the Western Front. Indeed, as an initial move, an officer from 9./KG 76 was assigned to KG 51 in order learn about the tactics used by the Me 262 unit and its experiences in combat.

Upon arrival at Münster-Handorf, Hauptmann Lukesch set about preparing the infrastructure for the imminent arrival of his *Einsatzstaffel*. In this regard, Handorf afforded him reasonable scope. A pre-war civil and military field, it had always been a dedicated base for bombers and long-range aircraft, and had plenty of hard surfacing, along with two concrete runways. A concrete perimeter road linked the servicing areas to the runways, and among its facilities, the airfield benefited from an efficient fuel supply system, communications, eight medium and large hangars, a hospital and a motor pool with garages.

The Ar 234s of the *Einsatzstaffel*/KG 76 would share Handorf with the He 219 nightfighters of I./NJG 1, another tricycle undercarriage aircraft that similarly benefited from the hard surfaces at the field. On 3 December Hauptmann Lukesch's deputy, Oberleutnant Arthur Stark, conducted an

inspection of a He 219 assigned to a training school at Burg with a view to the type being used as a preliminary training aircraft for the Ar 234 in preference to the existing Siebel Si 204 and He 111. With the exception of the engines, it was felt that there was a great similarity in operating, vision and flying characteristics, along with a tricycle undercarriage, although the He 219 was found to be easier to taxi than the Arado and required a shorter take-off run. It seems, however, that the idea was not advanced.

By late 1944 the flak defence at Handorf was viewed as sufficient, with guns positioned in towers and on rooftops around the field. Nevertheless, one of Lukesch's priorities upon arriving at the airfield was to reinforce the flak batteries, with additional 13 mm and 2 cm guns being obtained from a supply depot in Breslau – vital to protect the Ar 234s when at their most vulnerable to fighter attack during take-off, approach and landing.

Furthermore, Lukesch initiated the construction of several dedicated parking and blast shelters for the Ar 234s within woods at the edges of the airfield. These had the novel feature of hard, camouflaged roofs. Not only did this feature offer protection to the aircraft, but it also aided maintenance during the winter period. Additionally, each shelter was installed with a teleprinter and telephone connected to the *Staffel*'s *Gefechtsstand* so that changes to take-off times or delays in fighter cover could be communicated directly to the pilot at readiness.

Back at Burg, all efforts were made to ensure that each Ar 234 slated for use by the *Einsatzstaffel* was fitted with a brake parachute, *Lotfe* 7K and BZA 1B sights, rear-view periscope and mirror and the *Koppelnavigationsanlage* 3 dead reckoning navigation system. In addition, modifications had been carried out for the fitments of RATO units and auxiliary fuel tanks.

To accelerate instruction on the Ar 234, two Me 262B-1a two-seat trainers were delivered to Burg. Lukesch recalled;

'For the *Einsatzstaffel*, the pilots had already been selected. They came mainly from 9. *Staffel*, with some from 7. and 8. *Staffeln* and the *Gruppenschwarm*. Immediately after the arrival (*text continues on page 43*)

One of the *Einsatzstaffel*/KG 76's hard-roofed revetments at Münster-Handorf, photographed during an overhead inspection flight. Their shape and size was designed specifically to accommodate, protect and conceal an Ar 234 (*EN Archive*)

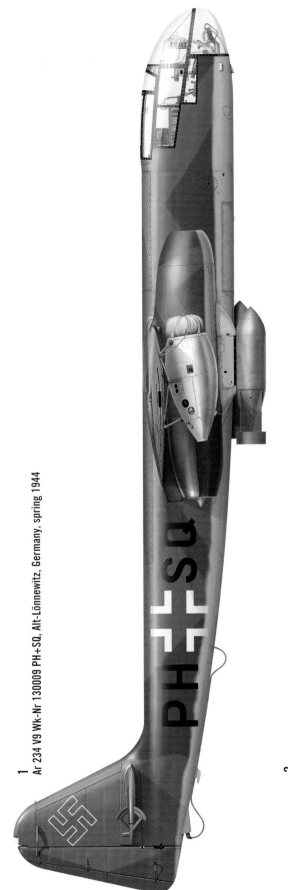

COLOUR PLATES

1
Ar 234 V9 Wk-Nr 130009 PH+SQ, Alt-Lönnewitz, Germany, spring 1944

2
Ar 234B-2 Wk-Nr 140325 F1+CS of 8./KG 76 and *Einsatzstaffel*/KG 76, Handorf, Germany, November 1944

34

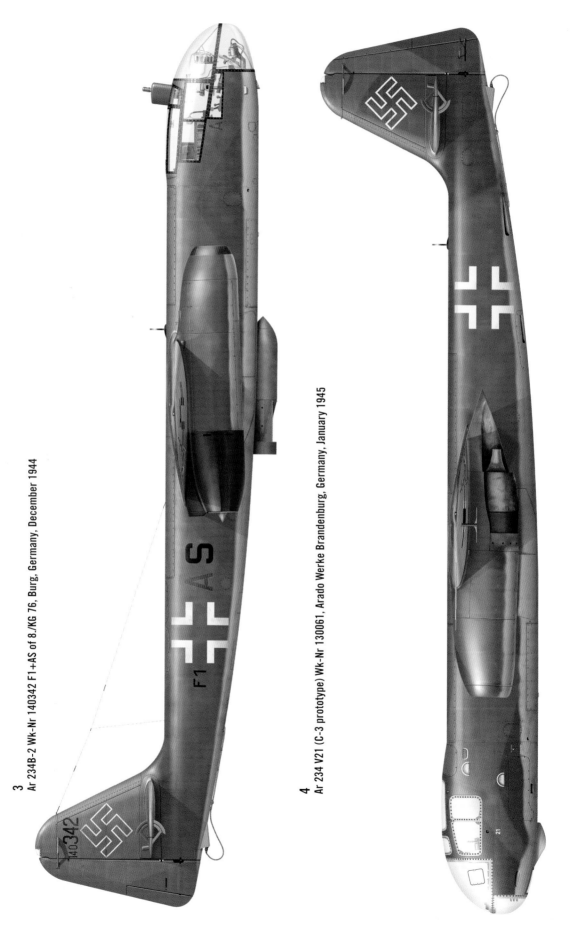

3
Ar 234B-2 Wk-Nr 140342 F1+AS of 8./KG 76, Burg, Germany, December 1944

4
Ar 234 V21 (C-3 prototype) Wk-Nr 130061, Arado Werke Brandenburg, Germany, January 1945

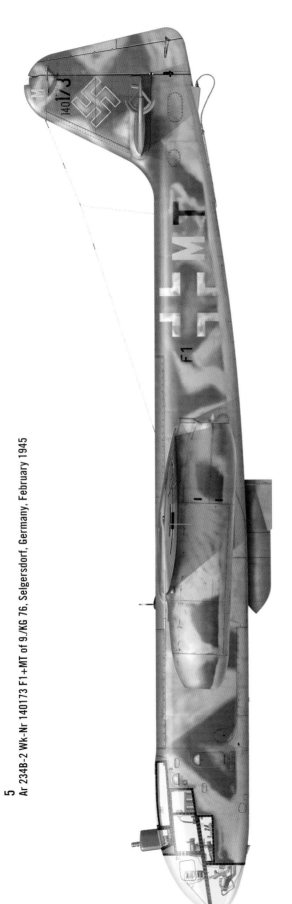

5
Ar 234B-2 Wk-Nr 140173 F1+MT of 9./KG 76, Selgersdorf, Germany, February 1945

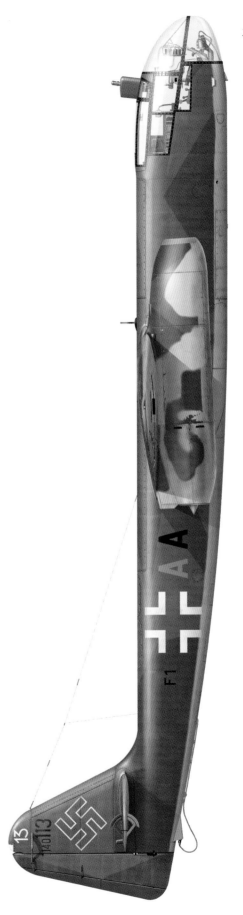

6
Ar 234B-2 Wk-Nr 140113 F1+AA of *Stab(?)*/KG 76, Flensburg or Schleswig, Germany, May 1945

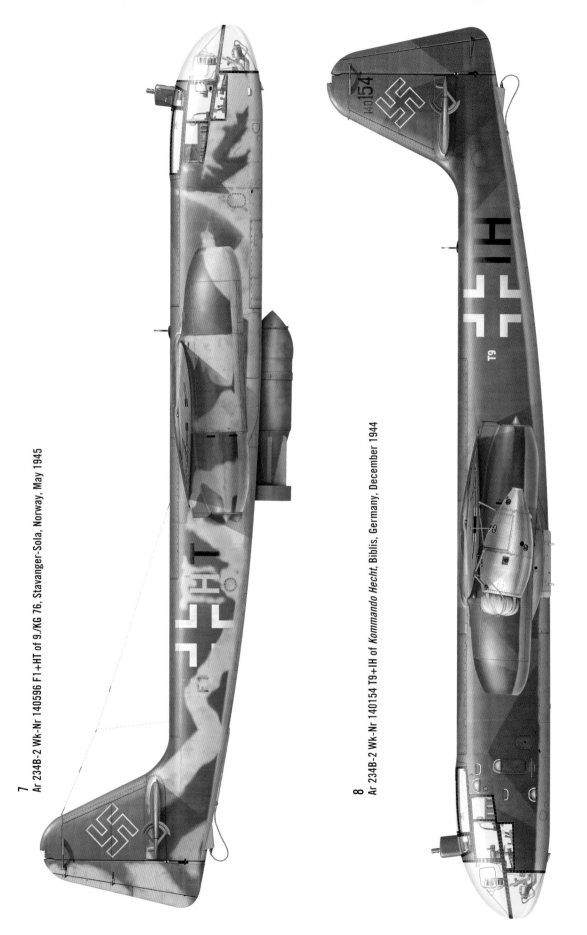

7
Ar 234B-2 Wk-Nr 140596 F1+HT of 9./KG 76, Stavanger-Sola, Norway, May 1945

8
Ar 234B-2 Wk-Nr 140154 T9+IH of *Kommando Hecht*, Biblis, Germany, December 1944

9
Ar 234 V7 Wk-Nr 130007 T9+MH of *Kommando Götz*, Juvincourt, France, July/August 1944

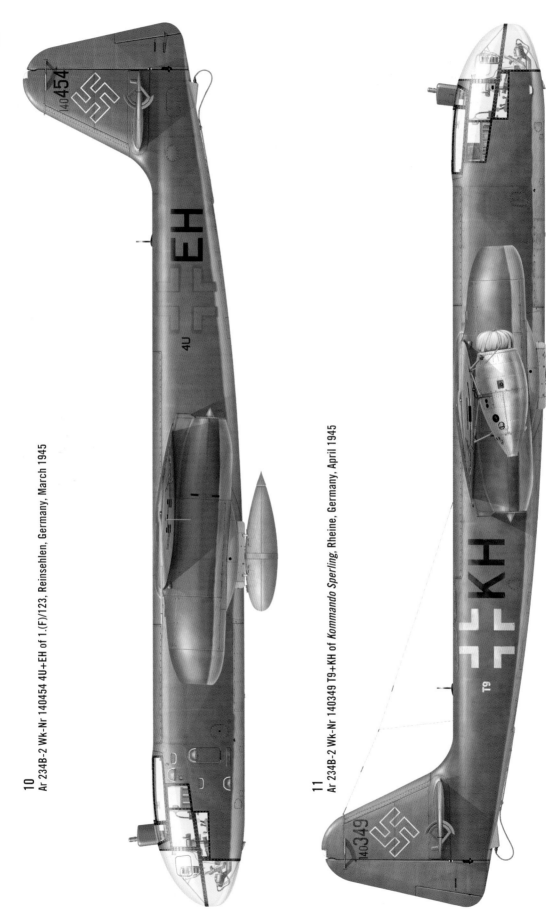

10
Ar 234B-2 Wk-Nr 140454 4U+EH of 1.(F)/123, Reinsehlen, Germany, March 1945

11
Ar 234B-2 Wk-Nr 140349 T9+KH of *Kommando Sperling*, Rheine, Germany, April 1945

12
Ar 234B-2 Wk-Nr 140611 T5+BH of 1.(F)/100, Lechfeld or München-Riem, Germany, April 1945

13
Ar 234B-2 Wk-Nr 140466 8H+HH of 1.(F)/33, Grove, Denmark, May 1945

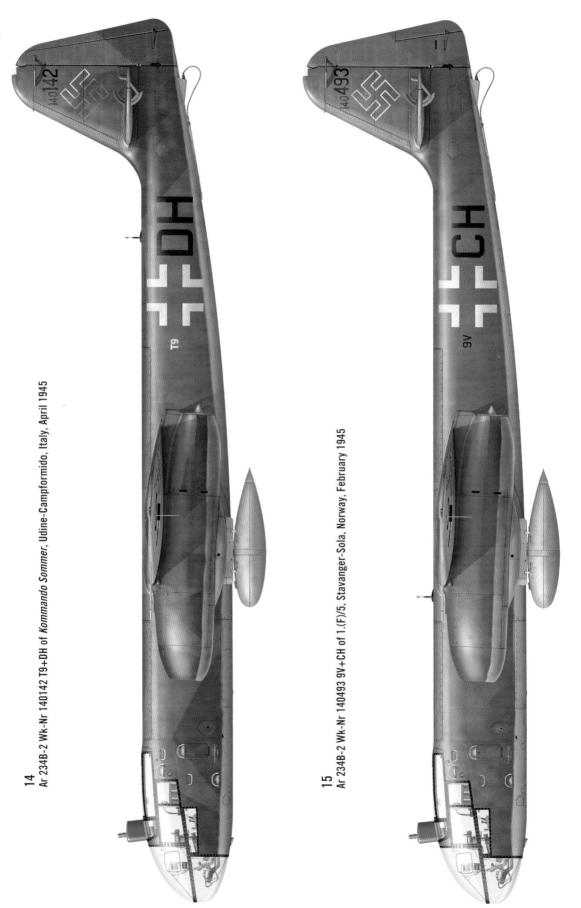

14
Ar 234B-2 Wk-Nr 140142 T9+DH of *Kommando Sommer*, Udine-Campformido, Italy, April 1945

15
Ar 234B-2 Wk-Nr 140493 9V+CH of 1.(F)/5, Stavanger-Sola, Norway, February 1945

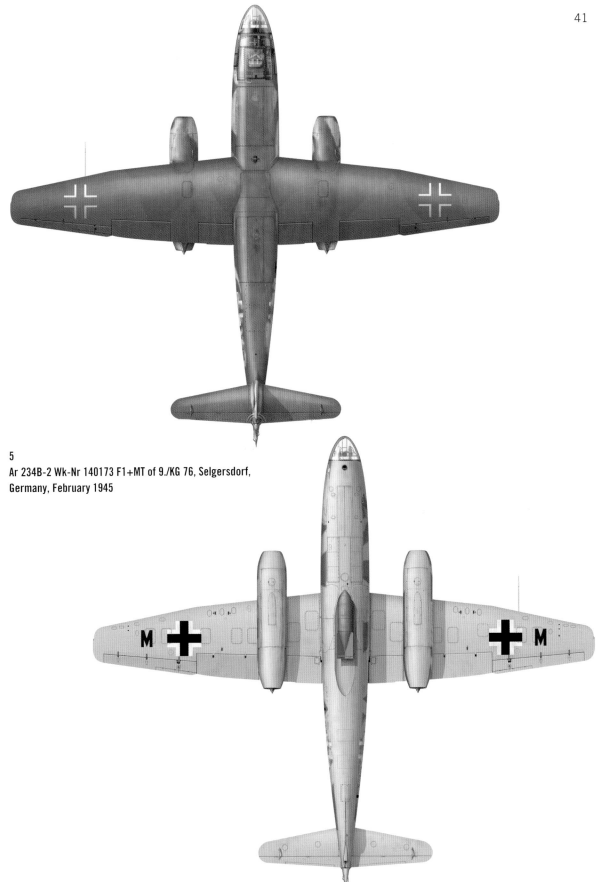

5
Ar 234B-2 Wk-Nr 140173 F1+MT of 9./KG 76, Selgersdorf,
Germany, February 1945

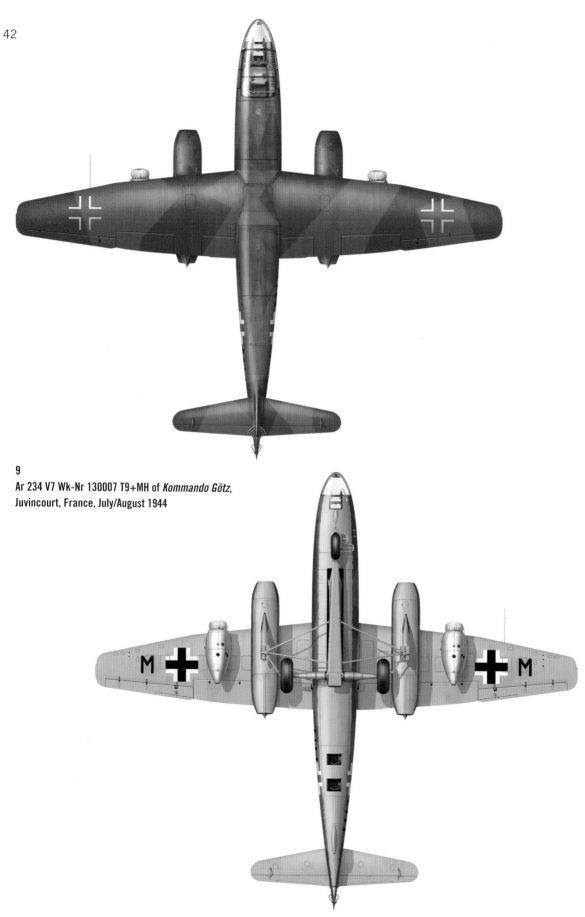

9
Ar 234 V7 Wk-Nr 130007 T9+MH of *Kommando Götz*,
Juvincourt, France, July/August 1944

of the first two-seater Me 262, followed later by a second, flying duties commenced. Up to five take-offs with this training model was sufficient to familiarise the pilots with the operation of jet engines and to make them accustomed to a nosewheel and high speed. The subsequent conversion on the initial Ar 234s then took place without any problem. Accidents naturally occurred, as the testing of this aircraft by industry had not been fully completed, and hence material and manufacturing faults appeared, resulting in mishaps.'

In addition to basic flying training, including take-offs, landings, single-engine and high-altitude flight, operational take-offs at maximum load, diving flights with and without practice bombs, RATO and twilight and night landings were all practiced. Much of this was hampered by autumn rain, which softened the landing grounds, compelling Oberstleutnant Kowalewski to instruct his pilots to land on runways rather than grass surfaces, particularly in view of the jet's fragile nosewheel, which was prone to buckling and collapse on soft ground if not handled correctly. In instances where the nosewheel failed to lower, it was better to land on a hard surface, for on soft ground there was the risk that shards of cockpit glazing could 'bury themselves into the earth like a spade', posing a severe risk to the pilot.

Ground conditions also increasingly caused problems for the small number of *Sonderkraftfahrzeug* ('special purpose vehicle') *Kettenkrad* motorcycle/half-track combinations used to tow the *Gruppe's* jets around their airfields. Although these vehicles had proved 'practical and reliable', they struggled to pull out aircraft that had sunk into the ground. The use of heavier, wheeled vehicles only exacerbated the problem, for they lost traction on the wet surfaces and makeshift 'paths' made of tree trunks. 'For towing the Ar 234 with tracked vehicles', reported Kowalewski on 18 November, 'a smooth, firm surface of stone or fine gravel is essential.'

During the period 11–18 November, III./KG 76 reported a daily average of 43 Ar 234s on strength, of which only four were serviceable – a significant drop from the previous ten-day period. These aircraft made a total of just seven starts and managed only three hours of flying time between them. In the period 19–30 November, III. *Gruppe* recorded an average daily strength of 54 Ar 234s, of which only 22 were serviceable. These aircraft made a total of 53 starts and amassed 33 hours of flying time.

One of III./KG 76's two Me 262B-1a two-seat trainers is refuelled at Burg. Note the bowser is coupled to a *Kettenkrad* semi-tracked tow tractor. The Messerschmitts proved well suited to the task of training would-be Ar 234 pilots (*EN Archive*)

Peak numerical strength during November came on the 20th, when there were 47 aircraft available for more than 50 pilots.

At the beginning of December, Major Heid relinquished command of III./KG 76 to Major Hansgeorg Bätcher, a renowned bomber pilot who had been decorated with the Oak Leaves to the Knight's Cross on 24 March 1944 following the completion of 655 combat missions. Bätcher clearly brought with him considerable operational experience, having joined the Luftwaffe in November 1935 and served in Poland and France with I./KG 157 and I./KG 27. He was then appointed *Staffelkapitän* of I./KGr. 100, with whom he served on the Eastern Front from July 1941, flying night raids against Moscow. On the night of 4/5 November 1941 Bätcher dropped an SC 1800 bomb on the Gorki vehicle works, scoring a direct hit.

By 1942 Bätcher was in the Crimea, flying over Stalingrad. He was appointed *Gruppenkommandeur* of I./KG 100 in June of the following year, after which he became the first bomber pilot to reach 500 missions. Having accumulated 600 combat missions by early November 1943, Bätcher departed I./KG 4 (which I./KG 100 had become) and joined the staff of *Luftflottenkommando 4*. His next operational posting would be with III./KG 76.

The highly decorated Major Hansgeorg Bätcher took over command of III./KG 76 in early December 1944, bringing his considerable operational experience to the *Gruppe*. He is seen here about to enter the cockpit of Ar 234B-2 'A' at Münster-Handorf in the winter of 1944-45. Note the large riveting of the cockpit framework and the clear vision panel at left (*EN Archive*)

During the early days of December 1944, III./KG 76 saw its strength rise to 52 Ar 234s, of which 22 were reported as serviceable on the 10th. Despite poor weather, the *Gruppe's* aircraft made 64 take-offs and its jets were airborne for a total of 38 hours. However, there was an element of 'robbing Peter to pay Paul', for although the *Geschwader* as a whole received 12 new Ar 234s during December, it had to relinquish 27 aircraft to industry, or to the *Luftflotte* or to other units. Five machines had been written off and four pilots killed, three of them as a result of accidents.

The low serviceability figure was due mainly to persistent issues associated with poor assembly of the aircraft, the resulting faults and problems with engines. Starting the latter in the freezing winter conditions became difficult because of fuel deposits on the cold walls of combustion chambers. At least one Jumo turbine unit failed as a result of the thrust nozzle covering rupturing at a welded joint. When dismantling the nozzle from another engine it was found to be congested with metal shavings and wool fluff. Additionally, the Riedel starter motors proved temperamental, with several breaking down after only a short period in use. It was also discovered that the suspension points on the RATO units often did not fit correctly to the wings.

An Ar 234 of III./KG 76 undergoes an engine change at Burg using a wheeled crane that has been rigged to the back of a lorry. With a mobile crane and associated equipment, a skilled team of mechanics could change an engine quickly, but much depended on the availability of replacement Jumo turbojets which were not always reliable (*EN Archive*)

Hauptmann Gerhard Morich, *Staffelkapitän* of 6./KG 76 and seen here wearing the Knight's Cross, stands in the centre of a line-up of pilots from his *Staffel* at either Alt-Lönnewitz or Hesepe in early 1945. There was considerable experience in 6. *Staffel*, which included several combat-seasoned bomber pilots and a handful of former instructors within its ranks (*Roger Gaemperle*)

Punctured tyres were also becoming a frequent occurrence, causing Arados to have to be withdrawn just before a flight when they burst while an aircraft was under tow from its dispersal. This was usually caused by sharp stones on the taxiways that then became caught in the wheel covers. *Einsatzstaffel* pilots also had to contend with misting of the cockpit glazing panels during take-off in cold weather – a problem compounded by the fact that the heating could not be turned on because of the resulting high fuel consumption.

The *Einsatzstaffel* took in ten new pilots on 18 December and had ten serviceable Arados. With operations imminent, the following day orders were issued to the effect that the *Staffel* would receive instructions and tactical directives from KG 51 under Major Wolfgang Schenck at Rheine. Both units would be placed under the ultimate control of *Lw.Kdo. West*.

Orders were also received to establish a second *Einsatzstaffel* drawn from personnel from Oberleutnant Kolm's 8./KG 76. The new unit would be equipped with the 15 Ar 234s that remained at Burg, most fitted with BZA sights, and, rather optimistically, 8. *Staffel* was to be brought to operational readiness by 31 December – by which time it was foreseen that a third *Staffel* would start to receive aircraft. This unit was to have been established from 6./KG 76 under Hauptmann Gerhard Morich, an experienced He 111 pilot, veteran of the *Blitz* against England and a recipient of the Knight's Cross. Morich stipulated that any pilot joining his new *Staffel* would need to display high levels of airmanship. Such qualities would be necessary to ensure survival in the coming weeks in skies that had become increasingly the domain of the Allied air forces.

On 16 December the last German offensive in the West, codenamed *Wacht am Rhein* (Watch on the Rhine) opened with SS-Oberstgruppenführer Josef 'Sepp' Dietrich's 6. *Panzer Armee* advancing into the fog-shrouded forests of the Ardennes. Essential to supporting the German attack was the need for the Luftwaffe to strike at the Allies' supply routes and hubs. The fog kept the air forces of both sides grounded until the 23rd, but at 2320 hrs that evening, orders arrived at Münster-Handorf from KG 51 at Rheine for the *Einsatzstaffel* to prepare for its first mission to be mounted the next morning. Its target was the Belgian city of Liège, an important Allied supply and rail transport hub. The *Staffel* was to carry out 'ongoing' attacks in 'acceptable' weather conditions, regardless of poor visibility – clearly, KG 51 had complete faith in the effectiveness of the Ar 234's PDS 11 and *Egon* equipment.

At around 0900 hrs on 24 December, Lukesch supervised the briefing of his pilots, while the groundcrews loaded bombs and checked and

prepared the turbojets. Nine Ar 234s were assigned to the mission, with each aircraft being loaded with an SC 500 High Explosive (HE) bomb filled with the composite TNT-based explosive Trialen. The pilots slated to fly that day, and their aircraft, were Hauptmann Lukesch (in F1+BT), Oberleutnant Friedrich Fendrich (F1+FT), Leutnant Eberhard Rögele (F1+ST), Feldwebel Wolfgang Stauß (F1+MT), Feldwebel Alfred Hachmann (F1+OT), Unteroffizier Rudi Zwiener (F1+HT), Unteroffizier Paul Winguth (F1+PT), Unteroffizier Helmut Sickert (F1+RT) and Unteroffizier Harry Thimm (F1+IT).

Major Hansgeorg Bätcher (left) in conversation with Oberleutnant Kolm, *Staffelkapitän* of 8./KG 76, at Burg in early 1945. In December 1944, it was planned to establish 8. *Staffel* as a second *Einsatzstaffel* at Burg with a strength of 15 Arados, although this never, officially, took place. Note the tow bar fitted to the Ar 234's nosewheel and the *Kettenkrad* used to tow the aircraft (*EN Archive*)

Lukesch took off at 1014 hrs and was quickly followed into the air by his *Staffel*. Having assembled into a line astern formation, they then flew from Handorf at low altitude across the snow-covered landscape towards Cologne, where they ascended to 500 m and headed for Bonn. Reaching that Rhine city, they continued towards Liège.

At one point during the outward flight, Lukesch spotted a lone Spitfire flying at 6000 m. Using his speed to approach the enemy aircraft from the right and behind, he moved in close enough to observe the pilot in his cockpit. 'He seemed rather bored', recounted Lukesch, 'shielding his eyes from the sun and looking for a short while at the ground as though he wanted to check his position. However, he suddenly turned his face towards me and then peeled off to the right, disappearing into the depths.' The Spitfire he encountered may well have been a photo-reconnaissance PR IX or XIX.

Reaching Liège just before 1050 hrs, the jet bomber pilots carried out what would become their standard tactic – a *Gleitangriff* (glide attack). This saw the Arados nose down gently from 4000 m to 2000 m, from which height they released their bombs. Over the target for ten minutes, two of the *Einsatzstaffel* pilots claimed to have scored strikes on the railway station, while Lukesch dropped his SC 500 on a factory and Hachmann bombed buildings in the city centre. Stauß apparently flew on to Namur, where he bombed rail targets.

Although enemy anti-aircraft fire was encountered, it was ineffective, probably because of the Arados' speed. The jets landed back at Handorf between 1124 and 1135 hrs. Only Winguth suffered a mishap when his landing gear partially failed and his aircraft received light damage to its wing. Nevertheless, the world's first jet bomber mission had been a success. 'As a *Störangriff* (nuisance attack)', Lukesch later reported, 'the attack achieved its purpose fully.'

In accordance with their orders from KG 51, the jets were back in the air that afternoon for a second strike at Liège. Lukesch almost had to abort when his F1+BT suffered punctures to both tyres during take-off, but he managed to climb away, followed by the eight pilots who had flown the morning's mission. On this occasion, when they encountered formations of enemy aircraft the Arado pilots boldly flew through them. At speeds of around 900 km/h, it seems they were so fast that the Allied aviators had no time to react, although with the enemy alerted to the presence of the Ar 234s, the German pilots had to drop their bombs with increased urgency. Over the target from 1530 hrs, they glided down through hazy skies from 2400 m to 2000 m, and the effect of their bombing was not observed. One pilot failed to release his bomb due to technical difficulties. All aircraft, including Lukesch's Arado with its burst tyres, landed safely.

Christmas morning dawned very cold and the mechanics rose early to warm up the turbojets, pipes, cables, rods and instruments ahead of the mission. Once again, the target for the day was Liège. Carrying one SC 500 apiece, eight Ar 234s led by Lukesch in F1+RT took off from Handorf at 0825 hrs, the formation being comprised of Oberleutnant Fendrich (F1+FT), Unteroffizier Thimm (F1+IT), Oberleutnant Saß (F1+CD), Leutnant Frank (F1+DT), Leutnant Rögele (F1+ST), Unteroffizier Eckerlein (F1+CT) and Oberfeldwebel Dierks (F1+NT). Oberleutnant Stark in F1+DD and Leutnant Dick in F1+KT were forced to abort their take-offs because of technical faults.

At 0900 hrs the eight Ar 234s appeared over Liège and bombed marshalling yards, station platforms and a freight shed in the city. A single bomb fell into houses east of the railway station, resulting in a fire, and another struck a factory. As the jets turned to head back to base, they ran into a formation of Tempest Vs from No 80 Sqn on morning patrol between Jülich and Malmedy. The fighters, led by Wg Cdr John Wray

Hauptmann Diether Lukesch, the commander of the *Einsatzstaffel*/KG 76, stands upright in the cockpit of his Ar 234B-2, F1+BT, as it is towed by *Kettenkrad* to or from its dispersal at Burg. At least two other pilots in flying overalls appear to be hitching a lift along with the groundcrew. Note the intake shields covering the Jumo 004 engines (*EN Archive*)

(Wing Commander Flying of No 122 Wing), were passing close to Liège when one of the RAF pilots spotted the German jets. Wray ordered one of his sections to break to starboard to attack and the other to break to port. Plt Off R S E Verran watched as one of the Arados dropped its bomb and then turn to the southeast, before making a wide turn to port and passing 200 yards in front of his Tempest V. Verran jettisoned his drop tanks, banked to port and opened fire, closing to 600 yards from behind. Staying on the Arado's tail, he fired several more short bursts, observing strikes on the port turbojet before he expended his ammunition.

Verran's victim was Ar 234 Wk-Nr 140352 F1+DT of Leutnant Alfred Frank, who then flew across the path of Wg Cdr Wray. The latter subsequently reported;

'As the enemy dived across in front of me and P/O Verran broke away from his attacks, I closed to 800 yards on his port side and fired one two-second burst, allowing three ring deflection, from which I saw one strike outboard of the port unit.'

Wray positioned himself behind the jet but was unable to close in from 800 yards out. He fired more bursts and watched the Ar 234 level out at around 90 m then pull away slowly towards the east. Although the attack by the two Tempest Vs had inflicted severe damage on Frank's left Jumo, he managed to keep flying for just over 30 minutes until he crash-landed near the village of Teuge, on the road between Apeldoorn and Deventer in the Netherlands. Frank had been fortunate to survive.

Early that afternoon, the *Einsatzstaffel* sent up eight Ar 234s to return to Liège, with Lukesch leading in F1+KT – it must have been repaired since the morning. Other pilots to fly were Leutnant Dick (F1+CD), Oberleutnant Stark (F1+DD), Leutnant Rögele (F1+ST), Feldwebel

Pilots of the *Einsatzstaffel*/KG 76 share a lighter moment possibly at Burg in the autumn of 1944. The *Staffel* commander, Hauptmann Diether Lukesch, is fifth from left wearing the *Krimschild* (Crimea Shield) on the arm of his tunic. Also seen here, from left to right, are Leutnant Werner Schmitz (Operations Officer), Oberleutnant Walter Saß (Technical Officer with the *Gruppenstab* assigned to 9. *Staffel*), Oberleutnante Eberhard Rögele and Friedrich Fendrich, Lukesch, Leutnant Alfred Frank (partly hidden), Oberleutnant zur See Böhmer (naval liaison officer) and (hidden) Oberleutnant Artur Stark (*EN Archive*)

Wg Cdr John Wray, Wing Commander Flying of Tempest V-equipped No 122 Wing, damaged Ar 234B Wk-Nr 140352 F1+DT of Leutnant Alfred Frank from the *Einsatzstaffel*/KG 76 on Christmas Day, the jet being wrecked in the subsequent crash-landing some 30 minutes later. This was Wray's third encounter with German jets, having previously downed two Me 262s (*CT Collection*)

Stauß (F1+MT), Feldwebel Hachmann (F1+OT), Unteroffizier Eckerlein (F1+CT) and Unteroffizier Zwiener (F1+HT). The jets flew over the Ardennes battlefront until they reached Bastogne, where they turned north and descended to an altitude of 3000 m. Despite heavy anti-aircraft fire, the Ar 234 pilots dropped their bombs at speeds of around 900 km/h on the railway station from around 2000 m, striking platforms, freight sheds, nearby housing and a factory, from which flames were seen to erupt. The Arados all returned safely to Handorf between 1503-1518 hrs, just over an hour after taking off.

From these initial missions, it was Lukesch's opinion that a glide attack using the BZA sight was the most tactically sound, and that with more missions over the front areas, levels of success could only improve.

On the morning of the 26th, six Ar 234s of the *Einsatzstaffel*, each loaded with an SC 500, attacked Verviers, a town taken by the Americans between Liège and Monschau. This time the jet formation was led by the *Staffel*'s Technical Officer, Oberleutnant Walter Saß (F1+CD), and comprised Unteroffizier Zwiener (F1+HT), Feldwebel Hachmann (F1+OT), Leutnant Rögele (F1+ST), Unteroffizier Winguth (F1+QT) and Oberleutnant Stark (F1+DD). Turning over Bonn, the jets, flying in close formation, descended from 5000 m to 1200 m and released their bombs, but results were not fully observed. All the Arados returned safely.

During the afternoon, Lukesch was at the head of six Arados as they attacked the road between Neufchâteau and Libramont, with Libramont railway station as a secondary target should no enemy traffic be seen. Unteroffizier Eckerlein (F1+CT) suffered a puncture on take-off but continued with the mission. Climbing at 500 km/h, the Arados passed over Bonn and then Trier, where they turned west. The road was found to be deserted, so the pilots bombed the railway station at Libramont, observing four hits on the target and two more on nearby housing.

A similar mission by seven aircraft to roads in the Neufchâteau and Libramont areas followed on the 27th, and on this occasion the *Einsatzstaffel* suffered its first fatal casualty when Leutnant Erich Dick's Ar 234 (F1+KT) veered off the runway during take-off, collided with a flak emplacement and burst into flames. It transpired that the pilot's vision had been impaired by the misting up of the cockpit glazing. Additionally, Oberfeldwebel Hachmann's F1+OT suffered a hydraulics fault and he was forced to turn back. The five remaining Ar 234s bombed positions held by the US Army's 28th Infantry Division and returned safely.

Lukesch led a second mission to Neufchâteau later that morning, comprising Fendrich (F1+ST), Zwiener (F1+HT), Sickert (F1+RT), Stauß (F1+MT), Hachmann (F1+OT), Dierks (F1+CD) and Winguth (F1+QT). Oberleutnant Stark and Unteroffiziere Thimm and Eckerlein experienced engine and mechanical problems, and were forced to abort.

As the Ar 234s returned to Handorf from what had been a generally successful mission, they were given the benefit of landing cover from a force of some 60 Fw 190D-9s from III./JG 54 based at Varrelbusch and led by the Knight's Cross-holder ace Hauptmann Robert Weiss. With such protection, Lukesch had instructed his *Staffel* to effect landing in the usual way. Within the space of 18 minutes seven of the Arados were down safely, but in the skies above the field turmoil was about to break out when a patrol of Tempest Vs from No 486 Sqn RNZAF led by future ace Sqn Ldr Keith Taylor-Cannon intercepted the Focke-Wulfs directly over Handorf. Taylor-Cannon took one section of Tempest Vs down to strafe the airfield just as the Ar 234 pilots were taxiing to a stop and climbing out of their aircraft. The last jet to return was F1+RT, flown by Unteroffizier Helmut Sickert, and as the enemy fighters swarmed around Handorf he was compelled to crash-land his aircraft – he was fortunate to escape without injury.

In the short, sharp firefight, No 486 Sqn shot down five Fw 190D-9s and damaged a sixth for the loss of one pilot and his Tempest V. III./JG 54 had prevented even worse carnage for the jets, and in his mission report Hauptmann Lukesch expressed his thanks to the *Gruppe* on behalf of the *Einsatzstaffel* 'for the good protection by our own aircraft during our landings on the second inward flight'.

For the next three days the weather closed in and prevented the Arados from flying. Then on the 31st, as conditions cleared, the *Einsatzstaffel* despatched ten Ar 234s, led by Lukesch, to bomb American troops known to be in woods north of Bastogne. As alternative targets, the jets were to attack roads around Eschweiler and the towns of Arlon, Neufchâteau and Liège. En route to their target, and with considerable air activity taking place on both sides, at one point the jets were compelled to fly through a formation of enemy twin-engined bombers under fighter escort, using their speed as their margin of safety.

Once pilots had reached their target, cloud prevented accurate bombing. The Arados duly dispersed, as arranged, to bomb the alternative targets. Lukesch dropped his SC 500 on American troops in the Bastogne area, only to be attacked by enemy fighters shortly thereafter. When one of them approached from head-on, Lukesch began a slow climb to evade the fighter as its fire passed behind him. The Allied pilot then chose to roll away, allowing Lukesch to escape unscathed. Another Ar 234 was damaged by

A mechanic sits astride the nacelle of the port side Jumo 004 in order to check the filler point for the annular oil tank of an Ar 234 at Burg (*EN Archive*)

enemy fighters, however. This may well have been the aircraft chased by aces Lt Col John Meyer and Capt Donald Bryan, both from the P-51D-equipped 352nd FG, who were patrolling near Verviers when they were alerted to the presence of enemy aircraft in the near vicinity. At one point Bryan was forced to break off his pursuit, but Meyer entered into a protracted chase that took him towards Bonn and the Rhine. As he later reported;

'Just west of Bonn, the enemy aircraft went back into clouds and I went under also, losing sight of him. I continued on this heading and again sighted enemy aircraft in a port turn at 5000 ft above the ten-tenths low cloud, with tops at 3000-4000 ft. I was able to close, and fired two two-second bursts at 700 and 600 yards, with 30 degrees deflection. I observed no strikes, but the enemy aircraft jettisoned its canopy (or escape hatch). To avoid going into cloud in a vertical bank, I broke off my attack and momentarily lost sight of him. A few seconds later, swinging around a small cumulus top of cloud, I saw the enemy aircraft headed straight down and into an overcast at 3000 ft. Circling the area, I saw another aircraft of the same type headed towards Cologne. I gave chase, firing several long bursts at extreme ranges, observing no hits.'

All the Ar 234s made it back to Handorf, however, although two returned with their SC 500s still attached.

By the end of its first week of combat operations, the *Einsatzstaffel*/KG 76 had executed nine relatively successful missions, deploying, on average, eight aircraft per mission. In total, the *Staffel* had mounted 68 individual sorties. Damage had been inflicted to the Arados on four occasions while landing, and this was recognised as the jets' weakest point operationally. One pilot, Leutnant Dick, had died as a result of non-combat injuries.

To herald the new year of 1945, under the codename *Bodenplatte* (Base Plate), at first light on 1 January the Luftwaffe mounted an audacious, large-scale, low-level ground-attack operation against 11 Allied fighter airfields in Belgium, Holland and northeastern France. Masterminded by the commander of II. *Jagdkorps*, Generalmajor Dietrich Peltz, the attack drew upon virtually the entire strength of the Luftwaffe's single-engined daylight fighter force on the Western Front (aircraft from 33 *Gruppen* were involved) and achieved near total surprise.

Immediately before the main attack, however, Peltz called upon the Ar 234s of the *Einsatzstaffel*/KG 76 to carry out two vital armed weather reconnaissance flights as close to the commencement of *Bodenplatte* as possible over the intended area of operations as far west as Antwerp. For this purpose, four jets had been fitted with obliquely mounted cameras.

Just before 0400 hrs, in darkness, the first two Arados, flown by Lukesch (F1+ST) and Stauß (F1+CT), took off and headed towards the front on what would be the first ever night mission for the Ar 234. They were followed an hour later by two more Arados flown by Fendrich (F1+HT) and Winguth (F1+OT). In clear skies, with visibility up to 40 km, the four jets flew over Nijmegen and then from Rotterdam to Antwerp, Brussels and Liège. Over the last two cities, the Arados dropped bombs, and upon their return their camera film cartridges were unloaded and their valuable contents quickly developed.

For his part, Lukesch was pleased with the way that his unit's first jet night flights had gone, and he believed that further such missions

A 1000 kg HE bomb loaded to the underside fuselage centreline of an Ar 234B-2. This type of weapon was expended only a few times by the Arados of KG 76, including against the Ludendorff bridge at Remagen in March 1945 (*EN Archive*)

could be carried out during periods of moonlight. He also expressed his satisfaction about the installation and performance of the *Reihenbildgeräte* (aerial mapping cameras), although the low temperatures did result in some malfunction when attempting to close the camera bay doors.

With the reconnaissance part of the day's activities successfully completed, the *Einsatzstaffel* quickly prepared for its contribution to the main attack – a strike on the Allied airfield at Gilze-Rijen, 15 km east of Breda in the Netherlands and home to RAF's No 35 Reconnaissance Wing of three squadrons of Mustang and Spitfires. The attack was to be carried out by ten Ar 234s in concert with the Me 262s of I./KG 51. Loaded with AB (*Abwurfbehälter*) 500-1D air-dropped containers, each holding 24 15 kg SD 15 *Splitterbomben* (fragmentation bombs), the intention was to 'pepper' Gilze-Rijen to such an extent that the subsequent movement of aircraft and vehicles would prove extremely hazardous.

The Ar 234s were ready shortly before 0900 hrs, although Lukesch was to be frustrated when the left Jumo 004 of his aircraft, F1+BT, failed during its take-off run. Two other jets suffered similar problems, while a tyre burst on another Arado, leaving just six aircraft to complete the mission.

The small, loose formation of Ar 234s climbed to 5000 m from Handorf and crossed over Arnhem. From Tilburg, the jets descended towards Gilze-Rijen for a *Gleitangriff*. They reached the airfield at 0932 hrs, flying across it in a single, high-speed pass at 1200 m and releasing their AB 500s upon what the German pilots estimated were

30 parked aircraft. Their ordnance was scattered over a wide area and some of the SD 15s exploded near the control building but caused little damage. A single Typhoon is believed to have been destroyed in the attack and others damaged, while three Ansons were also damaged and ten personnel injured or wounded. Despite the local anti-aircraft batteries reacting to the sudden appearance of the jets, the latter proved too fast. After conducting a quick assessment of the fighter attacks on the airfields around Antwerp and Brussels, all the Arados returned safely, five landing at Handorf and Thimm at Twenthe.

Many of the other units involved in *Bodenplatte* fared less well. Indeed, although around 300 Allied aircraft are believed to have been destroyed as a result of the attack, with another 180 damaged, and 185 personnel killed or wounded, 143 German pilots were killed or reported missing, including several formation leaders. In reality, the raid on Gilze-Rijen had little effect on the efforts of No 35 Reconnaissance Wing. Indeed, in assessing the operation, Lukesch noted, 'The impact of the AB 500s released over Gilze-Rijen is questionable since despite good efforts on the part of the pilots, no effects could be discerned.'

After *Bodenplatte*, for a brief time in January, the focus of the *Einsatzstaffel*'s efforts became the Antwerp area, and especially the port which continued to act as a vital hub for Allied supplies. Indeed, the night following *Bodenplatte* saw the Ar 234s carry out their second nocturnal mission – targeting the Antwerp docks and the main railway station in Brussels. Preparation for a night mission at least offered KG 76's groundcrews the respite of being able to undertake their fuelling and bomb-loading work on the runway with a much-reduced threat of attack by enemy aircraft. However, it was damage inflicted on runways by enemy air action that was also a perennial problem. That night two Ar 234s were forced to abort because of technical and runway-induced problems.

Thus, only four Ar 234s flown by Lukesch (F1+BT), Fendrich (F1+NT), Rögele (F1+ST) and Saß (F1+CD) proceeded to the target. Taking off at 2305 hrs, the pilots experienced searchlight beams and heavy anti-aircraft fire over the target. Nevertheless, they dropped their bombs into the illuminated area of the docks. Despite the hazards over the target, the Arado pilots felt that their speed would assist them in the event that they encountered a Mosquito nightfighter. Furthermore, thanks to the jets' PDS 11 three-axis course control equipment, the blinding effect of the searchlight beams in the glazed cockpits would be countered to some extent. Upon return from the mission, Lukesch once more commented 'night flying with the Ar 234B-2 in good weather conditions in the moonlight period is possible without difficulty'.

On the night of 2/3 January five Arados bombed the railway station at Mechelen, midway between Antwerp and Brussels, as well as secondary targets. It was a successful mission, with the aircraft releasing their ordnance over Mechelen, Brussels and Liège. Adverse weather again stopped further operations for the following two weeks, and amidst such conditions it was found that aircraft that were not able to be housed in the roofed revetments, or for which there were no spare tarpaulins, were vulnerable to the vagaries of heavy icing on wings and upper fuselage sections which was often difficult to remove.

Operations resumed during the afternoon of 14 January, although no fewer than six of the 11 Ar 234s assigned to attack enemy artillery positions north of Bastogne failed to take off. Lukesch remembered;

'I released the brakes of F1+BT at 1608 hrs and switched on the newly installed RATO units at a speed of approximately 80 km/h. Only the unit under the right wing fired, and I switched that off immediately. Nevertheless, the aircraft swerved some 40 to 60 degrees to the left, but I managed to bring it to a full stop within the manoeuvring area. Leaving the cockpit, I saw the same thing happen to the aircraft taking off next. It ran directly toward my F1+BT but fortunately stopped just before hitting it. The following four aircraft suffered the same fate. On inspection, we found a short circuit in the electrical wiring caused by the damp weather. From then on, the RATO units were only attached to the aircraft just before take-off, and no further mishaps occurred.'

The five remaining Ar 234s reached Bastogne and were over the target for ten minutes, dropping their bombs into an area of forest near the town, as well as on a road running south. The jets returned safely. The *Einsatzstaffel* remained on the ground for the next few days because of further inclement weather and the constant enemy air presence around Münster-Handorf. 'Very strong fighter activity over the field, with constant attacks', wrote Lukesch following the mission to Bastogne. 'Our own operations are only possible with our fighters protecting our take-offs and landings. Of 25 take-off protection fighters, only five reached our base, the others becoming involved in air combat on their way here.'

A wintry scene at Burg with a handful of Ar 234s of 8./KG 76 visible, including, in the foreground, F1+CS and F1+MS. The tail and rudder of Wk-Nr 140360 can be seen at right. In December 1944 the serviceable strength of III. *Gruppe* was usually around 20 aircraft (*EN Archive*)

For the rest of January, the *Einsatzstaffel* managed to make just two further attacks on Antwerp. On the 20th, five Ar 234s had to climb through a heavy snowstorm to reach the port. They then spent 22 minutes over the target, dropping their bombs on buildings in the dock area, although the effects were not observed. Heavy anti-aircraft fire followed the last jet to strike as the pilot made his bombing run.

On the 24th, in what would be its last mission from Handorf, the *Einsatzstaffel* was briefed to attack the Albert Dock in the Belgian port. Problems plagued the operation from the very start. According to Lukesch one jet dropped out because it had been 'waiting around for too long in a fully filled and loaded condition', while two others again suffered from failures with their RATO units. 'Because of one-sided thrust', wrote Lukesch, 'these aircraft swerved off the side of the runway and take-off was abandoned.'

Four serviceable jets, each loaded with a single SC 500 Trialen bomb, flew a westerly course through cloud and fog via Enschede and the Ijsselmeer, before turning south to Antwerp, which they reached at 0815 hrs. The Arados launched a glide attack, descending from 6000 m to 1500 m. One bomb fell in the northern dock, hitting and sinking the 5035-ton cargo vessel *Alcoa Banner* – two crewmen on board were killed. Others hit warehouses and a lock, causing fires. As the jets returned to Handorf, they were 'greeted' by what were identified as around 20 'P-47s'. Rögele's aircraft (F1+ST) was hit, although he was able to land unhurt. Once again, the presence of coordinated German fighter cover over the airfield prevented further losses.

In early February the Allies prepared to drive on the Rhine, and more than ever, the beleaguered German forces on the Western Front needed air support. On the 12th the *Geschwaderstab* of KG 76 left Burg for Achmer, arriving there seven days later. Here, it joined *Stab* III./KG 76 (with 8. *Staffel*, but minus 7. *Staffel*, which remained at Burg). At around the same time the *Einsatzstaffel* also relocated to Achmer from Handorf. Also at this point, Lukesch gave up command of the *Staffel* to take control of the operational training *Gruppe* III./*Ergänzungskampfgeschwader* 1 (as IV./KG 76 had been re-designated) from Major Karl-Hermann Millahn. Lukesch's technical and operational experience meant that he was the ideal candidate to oversee training on the anticipated four-engined Ar 234C-3.

The successor to Lukesch as *Staffelkapitän* of the *Einsatzstaffel* 9./KG 76 was Hauptmann Josef Regler, who had some 270 missions to his credit with KG 76 and who more recently had served as an instructor in IV. *Gruppe*.

Missions in early February were hampered by bad weather. Operations against Antwerp resumed from the 8th, but aside from this mission, involving a strike by seven Arados from, for the first time, 8./KG 76, they were immediately curtailed again. Weather prevented further missions until the morning of the 14th, by which time British and Canadian forces were opposite the fortified town of Kleve on the south bank of the Rhine.

From 14 February III./KG 76 commenced a series of missions against Allied troops, transport and armour in the Rhineland. Kleve lay between the Reichswald and a large flood plain close to the river. It was also directly in the path of advance of the British Army's XXX Corps. The terrain consisted of impenetrable forest that was difficult for Allied tanks to traverse. There were relatively few roads in the area, and those that did exist were narrow, covered in snow and unsurfaced.

Sixteen Ar 234s led by Major Bätcher bombed enemy troops in the morning, and they returned to Kleve during the afternoon for a second strike, although weather prevented accurate assessment of the bombing. Working in conjunction with the Me 262s of Hauptmann Hans-Joachim Grundmann's II./KG 51 based at Essen-Mullheim, no fewer than 21 Ar 234s from III./KG 76 attacked British and Canadian troops in the Bedburg area, 3.5 km southeast of Kleve. A second deployment saw 16 Arados bomb Kleve, Bedburg and the Reichswald, evading enemy fighters in the process. On the 22nd, the targets for nine Ar 234s were enemy columns around Aachen. During this mission Unteroffizier Zilaskowski had to bail out of his Ar 234 when it suffered an electrical failure and fuel shortage as a result of damage from enemy ground fire.

That afternoon, 14 Arados again bombed enemy columns near Aachen. Not far from the city, however, the recently appointed *Staffelkapitän* of 9./KG 76, Hauptmann Regler, was attacked by a P-47 flown by 1Lt David B Fox of the 366th FG. At first Fox thought that the Arado was an Me 262, but upon analysis of his gun camera film, he realised that this was not the case, and as he subsequently recorded;

'On our way home from a dive-bombing mission, I spotted a lone Ar 234 and used water [injection] to catch him. I dove on him, closing fast, and began shooting at about 50 to 60 degrees [off his tail] until I was in trail, when I ran out of ammunition. I observed strikes all over the plane. One large portion flew off, probably the canopy, and a fire started in the right engine. The plane went down smoking, and I followed it to the deck. Our own flak became so intense that we had to break off our pursuit. The plane continued a bit farther and finally bellied in'.

Regler's aircraft came down near the village of Selgersdorf, between Jülich and Düren, not far from the River Roer. The *Staffelkapitän* returned unhurt to Achmer two days later, and this was just as well, for III./KG 76 was about to enter its most intensive phase of air combat when it would need every one of its pilots.

Ar 234B-2 Wk-Nr 140173 F1+MT of Hauptmann Josef Regler, *Staffelkapitän* of 9./KG 76, sits in a field after crash-landing near Selgersdorf, five kilometres south of Jülich, on 22 February 1945. The aircraft is under guard by a US Army soldier, having been shot down by a P-47 flown by 1Lt David B Fox of the 366th FG. Regler's aircraft would be salvaged, dismantled and shipped to England, where it became the subject of close examination by the RAE at Farnborough (*Robert Forsyth Collection*)

CHAPTER FOUR

RECONNAISSANCE – 1945

Ar 234B T9+KH (Wk-Nr 140349) was strafed by Flt Lt Dick Audet of No 411 Sqn RCAF at Rheine on 23 January 1945, the burned out jet being found by Allied troops in April when the airfield was captured. By then the Arado had been fitted with fake nacelles and cockpit framing for use as a decoy (*EN Archive*)

The first photo-reconnaissance mission of 1945 was flown by *Kommando Sperling* during the morning of 1 January when Oberleutnant Werner Muffey took off from Rheine in T9+KH and overflew Volkel, Eindhoven, Brussels, Ghent, Maldegem, Antwerp and Gilze-Rijn. Later that same day the newly arrived Leutnant Häupel (T9+LH) undertook photo-reconnaissance of Eindhoven, Antwerp and Brussels. Clearly, the aim of these flights was to record the damage done to Allied airfields during *Bodenplatte*, and an aeroplane arrived that afternoon to collect the films taken by both jets.

In contrast to Rheine, Biblis was unserviceable on 1 January, as was *Kommando Hecht*'s T9+EH.

Decisions were being taken at this time on deploying full Ar 234 reconnaissance *Staffeln*. On the 1st, the *General der Aufklärungsflieger*, Generalmajor Karl-Henning von Barsewisch, noted in his diary that a new 1.(F)/123 would form from the long-inactive 3./Aufkl.Gr. (*Nacht*). The following day, his diary recorded that the new unit, along with 1.(F)/100, would support Army Groups B and G in the West. The former *Staffel* would join *Sperling* at Rheine, while the latter would be based in Biblis with *Hecht*, which was asked how many aircraft could be supported there. Both transfers could take place from the 15th, with the *Staffeln* subordinated to Major Richard Taubert's *Stab* FAGr. 123.

Around this time, von Barsewisch was also compiling a list of experienced pilot-observers suitable to fly the Arado. The *Kriegsmarine* was advised that by the end of the month a new Ar 234 *Staffel* should be covering England, with a *Schwarm* in Stavanger, Norway, to reconnoitre the ports and convoy routes between the Orkneys and Newcastle in collaboration with the *Befehlshaber der Uboote* (U-boat Command).

Although all five of *Sperling's* aircraft (T9+AH, T9+GH, T9+HH, T9+KH and T9+LH) were serviceable on 3 January, with every pilot ready for operations, the weather grounded them. Indeed, winter conditions appear to have prevented both *Kommandos* from operating from 2–12 January. On the 4th *Sperling* received a request from KG 76 at Münster-Handorf for photo-reconnaissance data on 'all targets suitable for bombing attack'. Somewhere between the 6th and 10th, T9+GH disappeared from *Sperling's* strength returns, reappearing on 12 January, then staying unserviceable for another week. A new machine, T9+CH, arrived on the 13th. T9+HH was declared unserviceable that same day and was not ready again for three weeks, which may reflect the mounting difficulties Luftwaffe units were having in obtaining spare parts.

Kommando Hecht could be said to have begun its transformation into 1.(F)/100 on 13 January, with Rheine reporting the arrival of two Ar 234s that would continue on to Biblis early the next morning, subject to a weather update. The number of signals exchanged between these two airfields on the 14th suggests such transfers took some orchestrating, what with fog, clearing snow from runways and incursions by Allied aircraft. It was 1035 hrs before 'Sperling 10' took off, followed 18 minutes later by 'Sperling 15'. Erich Sommer took off in T9+EH at 1145 hrs, although he was back on the ground before noon. A day later, *Hecht* noted the addition of two Ar 234s of 1.(F)/100 to its strength, so by the evening of the 15th the *Kommando* comprised T9+EH Wk-Nr 140344 (serviceable), T5+EH Wk-Nr 140310 (unserviceable) and T5+HH Wk-Nr 140315 (serviceable). 'T5' was the unit code of 1.(F)/100, while the *Werk Nummern* of the new aircraft explain the 'Sperling 10' and '15' signals, the final digits serving as call signs.

Three operations had been flown from Rheine on the 14th. Muffey (T9+KH) was aloft from 0903 hrs, carrying out coverage ordered a day earlier of the route Malmedy–Liège–Maastricht–Verviers–Sittard–Nijmegen, and new pilot Leutnant Günther Gniesmer returned early when T9+CH developed engine trouble. Muffey (T9+KH) was airborne once more from 1246 hrs, undertaking visual and photographic coverage of 'Position 2A'. There was no flying for several days following the 14th, and 19 January brought enquiries from Rechlin to *Sperling* about the effects of cold weather on the *R-Gerät*. That morning, 1.(F)/100's Oberfeldwebel Heibutzki (T5+HH) took off from Biblis, although unbroken mist and approaching cloud aborted his mission. *Sperling* was also busy;

'Hptm. Götz (T9+GH) – no success covering "Position E" on account of the weather.

'Lt. Häupel (T9+CH) – due to cover "Positions C and D", forced to divert to Bremen/Lemwerder after an air raid.

'Stabsfw. Seefeld (T9+AH) – covered "Positions A and B".'

Hauptmann Horst Götz's *Kommando* reported four or five pilots on strength throughout January, and at some stage Leutnant Wolfgang Ziese returned to 1./*Versuchsverband* OKL to help with testing of the Do 335.

An order from Göring was relayed on 20 January that if a jet made an intermediate landing at any airfield, technicians were to 'proceed at once to the pilot' and afford whatever assistance was needed. Instructions were included about which fuels were safe to use if no J2 was on hand. Generalmajor von Barsewisch noted in his diary the next day that 1.(F)/100's ground echelons had arrived in Biblis, and that T5+EH had been re-marked as T5+BH, perhaps to avoid confusion with T9+EH.

T9+AH was attacked by Spitfires while attempting a take-off on the 22nd, suffering severe fuselage and engine damage. Sqn Ldr Art Sager was leading the Spitfires of No 443 Sqn RCAF on an armed reconnaissance over the Münster–Rheine area at the time, and he later noted;

'[At 0930 hrs] Approaching the aerodrome on the NW outskirts of Rheine, observed a single-engine aircraft speeding down the runway, apparently about to take off. The Hun must at that moment have observed us, for he throttled back and started taxying off the runway. [I] attacked down sun, my No. 2 with me. Black splotches turned out to be a snow-plough, a truck, about 10 men and a twin-engined a/c. Gave about six seconds' worth of fire and was greeted in turn by intense light *Flak*. Unable to observe exact results but thought saw many strikes. Aircraft did not catch fire. I claim one unidentified twin-engined E/A damaged.'

T9+AH was still unserviceable on 2 March, and there was one groundcrew casualty.

Kommando Sperling was again targeted by Spitfires the following day (23 January), when the unit attempted five take-offs without success. While under tow to its dispersal around midday, T9+KH (Wk-Nr 140349) was strafed and burned out. The attack was described by Flt Lt Dick Audet RCAF in his combat report;

Flt Lt Dick Audet of No 411 Sqn RCAF destroyed Ar 234 T9+KH (Wk-Nr 140349) on the ground at Rheine on 23 January 1945. In his first ever aerial combat, on 29 December 1944, Audet had shot down three Fw 190s and two Bf 109s to become an 'ace in a sortie'. In all, he was credited with 11 victories, including an Me 262, before he was lost to flak while strafing a train on 3 March 1945 (*CT Collection*)

'While flying as Yellow One in 411 Squadron over aerodrome West of Rheine I sighted a/c lined up for take-off. I dived to attack but meanwhile a tractor hooked onto Me 262 [it was, of course, an Ar 234] and pulled it towards side of drome. I opened fire from about 1,000 yards. There were many strikes and a/c burst into flames about the starboard wing root. I fired again from about 300 yards, there was a sheet of flame all about the fuselage. I claim one Me 262 DESTROYED.'

The wreck was subsequently dressed up as a decoy and found when Rheine was captured by British troops on 2 April.

Also on 23 January, a message sent from Biblis referred to T5+CH and T5+GH, flown by Leutnante Franz and Schnabel, respectively. Leutnant Zeeb's machine, however, was marked K7+AL, suggesting 3.(F)/*Nacht* had 'baptised' it before becoming 1.(F)/123. By the following afternoon *Kommando Hecht* was reporting T5+BH unserviceable, but T5+CH, T5+GH and T5+HH were ready to fly alongside T9+EH and K7+AL (on the 28th *Hecht* explained that one of its machines belonged to *Versuchsverband* OKL and five to 1.(F)/100). The *Kommando* made a photo-mosaic of Luxembourg from 8000 m on the 25th and undertook visual reconnaissance of roads in Alsace-Lorraine. Two days later it apparently had similar orders, and it also created a photo-strip of the roads on some of the principal Ardennes battlegrounds, although by now the German forces had been pushed back to where they had commenced the offensive.

Gniesmer (T9+CH) made it into the air at 1330 hrs on the 26th, only to land within the hour after his four attempts at getting past Allied fighters ultimately yielded no photographs of 'Position 2A' thanks to the weather. The following day *Sperling* reported having four aircraft, plus one from 1.(F)/123 (an EH now appeared on the unit's strength, possibly 4U+EH). Some 142 technical, photographic and signals personnel had also arrived from the latter *Staffel*. On 29 January Gniesmer again took off in T9+CH, and when he had failed to return after three hours a search was mounted. Apparently, he was safe, for pilot strength was unchanged the next day. Gniesmer had, however, written off his Arado (Wk-Nr 140307) in an emergency landing near Neusustrum, 68 km north of Rheine, due to a shortage of fuel.

Perhaps responding to the recent Ar 234 losses, *Lw.Kdo. West* signalled on the 30th that 'With reference to *Einsatzkommando Götz* [message] No. 105 – order for fighter protection of *Sperling* at take-off and landing was given to II. *Jagdkorps*.'

News that T9+EH had suffered damage on take-off arrived on 29 January. Sommer had in fact flown the aircraft that afternoon, but it was declared unserviceable by both *Hecht* and *Sperling*. It seems Sommer flew it to Oranienburg, where, on 30 January, he received his posting to Italy. Also, T5+HH was unserviceable owing to ten per cent damage from enemy action, although no details were given about how this occurred. Meanwhile, *Hecht* complained that numerous spares were still lacking. A message was sent on the morning of the 30th that 1.(F)/100's Oberfeldwebel Windhövel and T5+GH had been stood down due to the weather. In early 1944, both this pilot and the previously mentioned Oberfeldwebel Heibutzki had flown the Me 410 with 2.(F)/122 in Italy. On the 31st, *Lw.Kdo. West* gave orders to '*Sonderkommando* 1.(F)/100 (Biblis)' for photographic coverage the following day of roads between Diekirch–St Vith–Bütgenbach–Monschau and Arlon–Bastogne–Aywaille– Liège–Maastricht–Sittard–Roermond.

Forty-eight hours earlier, *Lw.Kdo. West* announced that 'to guarantee the fulfilment of the allotted tasks in spite of enemy air activity in the area [of] Rheine, *Einsatzkommando Götz* is sending a detachment to Marx near Varel, in Oldenburg, [which is to act] as [its] advanced landing-ground. Designation *Sperling* 3.' The airfield was to be stocked with J2 fuel and the base commander made aware how urgent it was to support the detachment's work. Next day, *Lw.Kdo. West* agreed to the 'alternative occupation of Marx', confirming that supplies were being arranged, along with special signals procedures.

A query from *Kommando Hecht* was also answered – 'Alternative Detachment *Sperling* 3 set up today in Marx. It is possible to service two a/c there continuously.' At that time, *Sperling* only had T9+GH serviceable, as T9+AH had been out of commission for eight days after it was damaged by gunfire, T9+CH had crashed and T9+HH had also been unserviceable for 17 days, apparently with engine trouble. An aircraft could also be listed as 'unready for operations' when on detached duties, so if, as with '*Sperling* 10' and '15' (see above), '*Sperling* 3' was the last part of a *Werk Nummer*, then this Ar 234 was 140153 (T9+HH).

In early February, British intelligence reports on operational Luftwaffe airfields included 'Twin-engined, jet-propelled recce a/c (1 *Rotte*)' at Marx, although none appeared in photographs taken of the airfield on the 14th.

The *Kriegsmarine* recorded five days later that reconnaissance of ports, airfields and convoy routes in southeast England would fall to 1.(F)/33, initially equipped with six Ar 234s. *Lw.Kdo. West* decreed on 6 March that 'all 1.(F)/123's special tasks concerning recce of England' would lapse, with 1.(F)/33 (then at Wittmundhafen under Hauptmann Heinz Hattan) taking over. On the 22nd Hauptmann Götz signalled '*Kommando Sperling*, Marx' to ferry all flyable machines to Reinsehlen as soon as possible. The detachment was to be reduced to an *Einsatzkommando* for extreme range flights, calling on 1.(F)/33 for photographic interpretation and technical support.

Kommando Hecht, meanwhile, had been disbanded on 1 February, its tasks and much of its equipment being taken over by 1.(F)/100. T5+DH and T5+IH arrived at Rheine that same day, and they were soon repainted with 1.(F)/123's unit code 4U – perhaps because *Sperling* only had T9+GH serviceable that day, while 1.(F)/100 had four (ex-*Hecht*) jets ready for operations. The latter *Staffel*'s orders for the 1st were to photograph roads in the former 'Battle of the Bulge' salient in the Ardennes, plus others around Liège, Maastricht, Sittard and Roermond. Attention remained on the northern part of the front, and many of these objectives were assigned again for 3 February. Sommer was warned off returning from Oranienburg to Biblis until the 4th since the airfield was soft. Nevertheless, an Ar 234 supposedly marked KY+BL arrived there on the 2nd (probably K7+BL, sister to K7+AL).

T5+IH flew *Sperling*'s only mission of 3 February, Leutnant Viergutz taking off near midday for Nijmegen, Venlo and Roermond – his films were collected by a despatch rider that afternoon. The next day the *Kommando* was augmented by T5+BH and T5+CH, one of which was perhaps KY+BL repainted, while the other was Wk-Nr 140464 – a sortie was flown over Holland by one of these aircraft that morning (4th).

The diary of the office of *General der Aufklarungsflieger* noted for 4 February that *Kommando Sommer* was to transfer by rail to Osoppo for operations in Italy – the first known mention of that unit name and destination. On the evening of the 7th, 1.(F)/100 reported that Wk-Nr 140344 (Sommer's T9+EH) had reverted to the *Versuchsverband*. The latter also announced its own transfer to Kaltenkirchen, and that Sommer must obtain other units' vehicles 'for your transfer to Osoppo' – lorries were scarce and the issue was still 'live' ten days later. Some 320 cubic metres (320,000 litres) of J2 was already in Italy, however, and the 9 February

Luftwaffe disposition map notes alongside Osoppo that *Kommando Sommer* is on its way.

Three days earlier, on the 6th, Wk-Nr 140460 had been delivered to Rheine, and other developments followed on 7 February. The designations *Sperling* and *Hecht* were cancelled with immediate effect in favour of 1.(F)/123 and 1.(F)/100, and the latter was asked if its *Staffelkapitän*, Hauptmann Hermann Holert, could safely land at Biblis. 1.(F)/123's assignments for the 7th included coverage of the frontline in Holland and northwest Germany to a depth of ten kilometres on the Allied side, the Scheldt and Humber estuaries, Hull and the effects of V-weapons on London.

On 8 February, Götz ferried T9+GH to Oranienburg, after which the long-serving *Staffelkapitän* was replaced by Hauptmann Hans Felde, who would take over command of 1.(F)/123. That morning, sorties were flown by Oberfeldwebel Küpper (4U+BH), Felde himself (4U+DH) and Viergutz (4U+IH), although the latter was thwarted by the weather. For its part, 1.(F)/100 had been directed to photograph roads in Alsace-Lorraine and Luxembourg. On the 9th only a 39-minute weather reconnaissance was flown, and on 10 February a solitary Ar 234 was unable to carry out its mission owing to continual fighter attacks. On the 11th two missions over Holland were aborted by bad weather, although Felde flew to the Humber during the morning. Nearing Rheine, he was stalked through clouds by Tempest Vs of No 274 Sqn led by Sqn Ldr David Fairbanks, who later reported;

'We carried on for about 15/20 miles and evidently he thought he had lost us. As I came through a small patch of cloud I saw the E/A about 800 yards dead ahead at approx. 1500 ft over Rheine A/fd. He was just dropping his nosewheel and started to turn to starboard. I dropped my tanks and closed to approx 250–300 yards, firing a ½-second burst to test my deflection. I saw little puffs of smoke on the fuselage and then a great burst of flame. The E/A went straight down immediately and blew up in the centre of Rheine A/fd. I claim 1 Me 262 destroyed.'

Three Arados had now been destroyed at Rheine by RCAF pilots (although Fairbanks was American by birth), and Felde killed. The latter's machine that day was 4U+DH, its *Werk Nummer* generally given as 140149, although in March 1.(F)/100 quoted that number for its T5+AH.

The 14th saw two pilots – Oberleutnante Krüpe (4U+EH) and Muffey (T9+HH) – airborne within four minutes, both bound for Holland. A sortie was also flown that afternoon by Oberleutnant Planck (4U+EH), taking in Antwerp–Deurne, while 1.(F)/100 despatched two machines to eastern France (T5+AH flown by Leutnant Zeeb and T5+CH flown by Oberfeldwebel Windhövel). The former encountered heavy anti-aircraft fire over Metz

American-born Sqn Ldr David 'Foob' Fairbanks was leading the Tempest Vs of No 274 Sqn on 11 February 1945 when they encountered the Ar 234 of Hauptmann Hans Felde and shot it down over Rheine. Fairbanks would end the war as the top-scoring Tempest V ace (*CT Collection*)

and Sélestat and the latter was unsuccessfully attacked by three Mustangs near Metz, forcing him to abandon his mission. Nevertheless, Zeeb had taken good photographs of the airfields at Metz and Nancy-Essey. By the 14th 1.(F)/100 had seven Arados on strength, four of them serviceable.

On 15 February three sorties were flown to Malmédy–St Vith–Metz, although one Ar 234 turned back with technical problems and the remaining two ran into bad weather that curtailed their missions. Three days later, low production of J2 prompted this OKL directive;

'It is absolutely forbidden for [jet] aircraft to taxi under their own power prior to take-off and after landing and also to and from their parking places. Remember that an Me 262 consumes 200 litres of J2 while taxiing for five minutes. Arrange for the strictest supervision of flying.'

The previous day, *Kommando Sommer*'s vehicles and equipment had been loaded onto a train and were barely underway when American fighter-bombers attacked near Worms, destroying 80 per cent of the unit's gear. *Lw.Kdo. West* urgently directed *Kommando Götz* to prepare for transfer to Italy instead 'with personnel and equipment, but without aircraft. 1.(F)/123 will take over the former tasks of *Kdo. Götz*'. Oberleutnant Sommer was to remain in Biblis, pending a new assignment. On 19 February Götz completed his handover to 1.(F)/123 and his unit was ready to move to Italy two days later.

However, 1.(F)/123 needed to replace the recently killed Hauptmann Felde, and Götz was duly appointed. Higher authority now decided that the new *Kommando Süd* (South) should comprise a *Kommandoführer* and three pilots. All would need experience of operations in the West, and they were to be drawn from 1./*Versuchsverband* OKL.

A small advance party had by now arrived in Osoppo, only to discover that nothing was known there of any plans for the deployment of Ar 234s. Of the assigned pilots, Leutnant Günther Gniesmer reached Lechfeld on 21 February, Stabsfeldwebel Walter Arnold reached Riem the next day and the ground echelon entrained at Münster-Handorf on the former

Kommando Sommer lost 80 per cent of its equipment when its train was attacked by Allied fighter-bombers shortly after getting underway for Italy on 14 February 1945 (*EN Archive*)

date. It was also announced that Oberleutnant Werner Muffey would fly Ar 234 T9+HH to Lechfeld and thence on to Osoppo as leader of *Kommando Süd* – Muffey knew nothing of this, as he confirmed to one of the authors in 1990.

Despite plans for Sommer to take over 1./*Versuchsverband* OKL at Kaltenkirchen, he was again given the Italian command. By 26 February the first Ar 234 had arrived in Osoppo according to a Luftwaffe document, although Italian fighter pilot Capitano Mario Bellagambi wrote in his diary for the 23rd, 'A *Turbin Jäger* [jet fighter] has arrived.' It was only on the 28th that Gniesmer signalled Sommer to say he had finally arrived 'here' – presumably Osoppo – and that everything was prepared.

Nine days earlier, on 19 February, 1.(F)/100 had sent an Ar 234 to reconnoitre roads between Alsace and Düren (threatened by the US First Army). On the 21st, the unit's Oberleutnant Walter Carlein took off in T5+BH in an attempt to photograph aerodromes around Metz and Verdun, but he was frustrated by weather and technical problems. The following day, 1.(F)/123's Oberfeldwebel Schiffels (4U+CH) photographed Dutch targets. However, the unit's Oberleutnant Krüger (4U+EH) suffered engine damage. Finally, 1.(F)/100 successfully covered 350 km of frontline between Drusenheim and Düren on the 22nd.

1.(F)/100 was particularly busy on 23 February, with Hauptmann Holert (T5+HH), Leutnant Beck (T5+GH), Feldwebel Haider (T5+FH) and Stabsfeldwebel Gildemeister (T5+AH) all flying. Beck and Haider were only partially successful, the former meeting cloud over eastern France and the latter losing his way while evading fighters. The following day, there was a 135-minute flight by 1.(F)/123's Oberleutnant Bruno Radau (4U+BH), taking in the Thames Estuary, Ramsgate, Dover, the Scheldt Estuary and Antwerp. The *Staffel*'s Oberleutnant Krüger (4U+EH), meanwhile, carried out a photo-reconnaissance of Venlo, Aachen and Hasselt. That day's weather permitted only one sortie by 1.(F)/100, however, Oberfeldwebel Puls (T5+FH) reporting 'task as ordered [yesterday], only partially carried out owing to fighter defence'. 1.(F)/100 had by then attained a strength of ten aircraft (four of which were serviceable) and 11 operational pilots.

The Ar 234 was now also operational in Norway, with the *Kriegsmarine* reporting on 25 February that one was to take off from Stavanger at 1500 hrs, fly out over the sea and return after 30-45 minutes. The following day the official diary of the *General der Aufklärungsflieger* noted that *Einsatzkommando* 1.(F)/5's ground echelons were in Stavanger, along with a single Ar 234, and two more would fly in from Grove, in Denmark, given favourable weather. On 28 February an Ar 234 from 1.(F)/123 ran short of fuel and was forced to break off reconnaissance of the Humber Estuary after finding a 20-vessel convoy near Grimsby.

On 1 March, the Luftwaffe's commanding general in Denmark, Generalleutnant Alexander Holle, proposed moving *Stab* FAGr. 1 to Grove and bringing 1.(F)/1 there from Neubiberg. In the event the *Stab* went to Wittmundhafen on the 9th. After practice flying, Stavanger's Ar 234s were expected to be operational from 10 March, the *Kriegsmarine* being told that they would carry out reconnaissance of northeast English coastal waters in support of the U-boats' 'inshore campaign' which introduced the Type XXIII boat with greatly improved underwater performance but just two torpedoes.

Further south, 1 March brought a report to Germany about the strength of units in Italy, including 'Special Staff Götz' with one pilot and an unserviceable Ar 234B-2, for which 382 cubic metres of J2 were available. As previously noted, Sommer was meant to join the Arado unit in Italy, but on 4 March he was ordered to Kaltenkirchen instead. That same day, Oberfeldwebel Lüders signalled from Lechfeld that his advance party had arrived at Osoppo on 16 February, but not the aircraft, and operating conditions at the Italian airfield were not yet known. If he had indeed been in Lechfeld for a fortnight, Lüders should have learned by then that Gniesmer had been and gone. It appears, therefore, that he was still expecting more than one aircraft – presumably those of the designated *Kommandoführer* – and the fourth pilot whom Götz had told Sommer would complete the flying staff of the new *Kommando*.

1.(F)/123 asked 1.(F)/100 at midday on 9 March when Sommer would leave for Lechfeld. The prompt reply was that he had flown in the previous day, and would probably leave on the 13th. This signal concluded 'column not yet ready for transport, has lorry left Ibbenbüren?' (about 15 km east of Rheine, but almost 400 km from Biblis). Since men and equipment of *Kommando Götz* had been put aboard a train from Münster to Italy almost three weeks earlier, evidently something was still lacking. Sommer recalled to one of the authors that his unit's gear had gone by road under Oberleutnant Manfred Mähnhard of the *Versuchsverband*.

No documentation survives, but Sommer recollected visiting Oranienburg on 10 March, where his aircraft was fitted with a ventral gun pack by the Ar 234 nightfighter trials detachment. The next day he went by car to report to von Barsewisch at Würzburg and, returning to Oranienburg (a 1000 km round trip), had the Arado's gunsight calibrated on the 12th. It is not clear what led Sommer to have the weapons installed after flying unarmed Ar 234s in the West for six months – the paucity of friendly fighters to cover take-offs and landings in Italy, perhaps?

According to Arnold's logbook, he flew from Lechfeld to Udine on the morning of 13 March. Oranienburg was notified that Sommer had flown from Biblis to Lechfeld and Osoppo on the 14th, his *Kommando* now consisting of his own Wk-Nr 140344 T9+EH, Leutnant Günther Gniesmer's Wk-Nr 140142 T9+DH and Stabsfeldwebel Walter Arnold's T9+FH (*Werk Nummer* unknown).

OKL intended them to take over from 2.(F)/122's Me 410s and (in part) from NAGr. 11's Bf 109s. 1.(F)/22 was to deploy to Italy by the end of April and absorb the *Kommando*, its personnel having left Norway on 21 January for Ar 234 training and re-equipment at Jüterbog-Waldlager – Hauptmann Fuchs had been appointed *Staffelkapitän* on 6 March. 1.(F)/22 never got to Italy.

Arnold logged a flight from Udine to Ancona and San Benedetto on 15 March. This was possibly the *Kommando*'s first operation, but the authors cannot corroborate any of his claimed Ar 234 sorties from wartime sources. More reliably, the *General der Aufklärungsflieger*'s diary noted on the 17th that *Kommando Sommer* was ready for operations in Udine, without explaining the switch from Osoppo. Sommer later wrote that, visiting the latter airfield the day after reaching Italy, he found it 'still not fit for us'. At Udine-Campoformido and Lonate Pozzolo, however, there were specially trained groundcrews, blast pens and camouflage netting. Distrusting the telephone system, Sommer used the code numbers '986' to report an Ar 234 take-off. The *Kommando* depended on FAGr. 122 and NAGr. 11 for photographic facilities.

Back at Rheine, 1.(F)/123's assignments from *Lw.Kdo. West* for March had been photographing the Humber Estuary, southeast England and harbours from Hull to Dover, including the Thames Estuary, and coverage of V-weapon damage in Antwerp. In a 2½-hour flight on 2 March, Oberleutnant Radau (4U+BH) found only small craft in The Wash and adjacent estuaries. That same day, Leutnant Viergutz (4U+IH) abandoned his mission with a damaged engine, while Oberfeldwebel Jorek (4U+CH) was kept from photographing Antwerp by the weather. The *Staffel* had seven Ar 234s (four serviceable) and 14 pilots (12 fit for duty) on the 2nd.

On 2 March, 1.(F)/100 attempted, unsuccessfully, to locate Allied tank and artillery concentrations east of Saarburg. Its strength fell from ten Ar 234s (four serviceable) to eight (four serviceable) between the 2nd and 3rd, with ten pilots operational.

With the Allied armies closing up to the west bank of the Rhine, 1.(F)/123's missions became increasingly directed towards obtaining warnings of where crossings might be attempted. In the event, the first of these – by the US Army at Remagen on the 7th – took the Germans by surprise. On 9 March, Oberfeldwebel Küppers took off at 1120 hrs to cover the river's left bank from Nijmegen to Köln, but he had not returned by evening (4U+CH disappears from subsequent strength returns). Oberleutnant Krüpe was in the air several hours later that afternoon, although ten-tenths cloud at 3500 m precluded photography.

On the 8th, 1.(F)/100's Oberfeldwebel Windhövel (T5+GH) photographed airfields in eastern France, but had no luck with either the Remagen bridgehead or a US Airborne depot at Sissonne, France. The next known 1.(F)/123 mission was a visual reconnaissance of the Koblenz area (now threatened by the US Third Army) on the afternoon of 12 March. The following morning Oberleutnant Merk (4U+MH) aborted after only 24 minutes owing to bad weather. These conditions also prevented 4U+HH fulfilling a 'special task' for 14.*Fliegerdivision*.

A 1.(F)/100 machine managed to photograph airfields in Belgium and Holland (well north of the unit's usual beat) on the 13th, while a second aborted with damaged landing gear, and another broke off coverage of the frontline and central Rhine following a technical breakdown. 1.(F)/100 reported a strength of eight Ar 234s (three serviceable) and 12 pilots the following day, when one of its aircraft undertook a photo-reconnaissance mission of roads in the Remagen–Bitburg–Trier–Koblenz area and the American-held left bank of the Rhine. An attempt to get similar coverage of the left bank between Koblenz and Sinzig was defeated by nine-tenths cloud, however.

On 14 March, 1.(F)/123's Oberleutnant Merk twice tried unsuccessfully to photograph airfields round Rheims to locate Allied air transport units. Weather ended the first attempt and the Arado's fuselage was damaged taking off for the second (4U+MH was unserviceable that evening). Missions to Belgium and Holland on the 15th fared no better, with two being curtailed by technical failures and two aircraft reportedly forced down and damaged after encounters with opposing fighters, although neither pilot was hurt. 4U+HH was unserviceable the next day and 4U+AH was absent from the order of battle for more than two weeks.

During this period, 1.(F)/100's Stabsfeldwebel Gildemeister (T5+AH) and Oberfeldwebel Windhövel (T5+CH) successfully covered French airfields and the Remagen bridgehead (on the 17th). Yet again, other sorties were hindered by the weather.

On the 19th *General der Aufklärungsflieger*'s diary noted that Oberleutnant Sommer had flown an operation in Italy, and Allied pilots reported 'two Me 262s' north of Udine. Coverage was obtained of Livorno, and the following day an Ar 234 flew from Udine to Lonate at dawn. It took off on an *Einsatz* (mission) from the latter airfield just 90 minutes later, photographing shipping in the port of Ancona. Following such 'intermediate landings', Sommer recalled groundcrew towing the Arado out of sight, fitting dummy airscrews to its nacelles and topping up the tanks. Nevertheless, the Ar 234s were occasionally caught up in strafing attacks on Italian airfields by USAAF fighter-bombers. One such mission was undertaken by the P-47-equipped 79th FG, as noted in the following entry from the group's reports on operations;

'The highlight of the month was the attack on Campoformido A/D [on] March 20th . . . A new sortie record – 260 – in 24 missions. Destruction thundered on the A/D as 8,480 x 20 lb frags, 141 X 100 WPs [white phosphorus], 1,233 rockets and 3,970 rounds of 0.50-calibre ammunition rained on the runways, revetments, buildings, gun positions, etc. . . . Total claims [were] 21 aircraft damaged and destroyed.'

Sommer recalled attacks all day on 20 March by fighter-bombers. In the dispersal pens, rockets set a Bf 109 afire and its exploding ammunition damaged his Arado, which took a day or two to be repaired. A jet did fly, with cover from six Bf 109s from the Italian 4ª *Squadriglia* from Aviano. As late as the 27th *Kommando Sommer* was trying to sort out what should become of some of its equipment and personnel still stuck in Germany.

The 20th had also seen an Ar 234 of 1.(F)/123 undertake a photo-reconnaissance of the Rhine from Nijmegen to Düsseldorf. An operation was also flown the following morning, although Oberfeldwebel Jorek was hindered in photographing Xanten–Appeldoorn by 'continual fighter attacks'. 1.(F)/100's Arados flew two missions on the 21st over Bingen, Mainz, Ludwigshafen, Koblenz and Kochem, apparently to establish the progress of American forces. Allied advances to, and over, the Rhine were forcing the Luftwaffe to withdraw from threatened bases, and with Biblis just five kilometres from the river's eastern bank, 1.(F)/100 pulled back to Schwäbisch Hall. Its new home, however, was expected to be unserviceable until the 28th or 29th.

Also on the move was 1.(F)/123, as Oberleutnant Muffey recalled;

'We transferred our ground staff from Rheine to Reinsehlen on 23 March but admittedly we had some trouble finding an appropriate replacement for Rheine in view of the rapid progress of the Allied troops and Kaltenkirchen had been one of a couple of candidates we had to choose from.'

On 25 March 1.(F)/123's Oberfeldwebel Jackstadt (4U+HH) logged a reconnaissance mission from Reinsehlen, covering the Rhine from Emmerich to Duisburg. Two days later, the *Staffel* was down to five jets (three serviceable), although it had received two new ones – 4U+DH and 4U+LH – by the end of the month. On the 31st, Oberleutnant Fritz Worschech (4U+EH) made a forced landing at Bispingen, 60 km south of Hamburg, owing to engine and control failure. He was slightly injured and his Ar 234 was 90 per cent destroyed in the crash and ensuing fire, although the *Staffel* had a new 4U+EH within a week.

In Norway, two Ar 234s had taken off on the afternoon of 23 March and the one on the 'southern task' obtained photographs of coastal waters from the Firth of Forth down to South Shields. The 'northern task' fell to Leutnant Hellmut Hetz, his 9V+AH (Wk-Nr 140341) needing drop tanks to make the range – the heavy jet required rocket-assistance to get off the ground. Making landfall north of Aberdeen, he headed towards the Firth of Forth until a fuel leak and an overheating engine led to the flight being aborted and Hetz returning to base. He was badly hurt in the forced landing which ensued, and his aircraft seriously damaged.

Both of these sorties were reported to the *Kriegsmarine* by 1./FAGr. 1, which the Allies had not known was in Norway, let alone equipped with jets. Under this new designation, the same pilots and Arados, in the same markings, continued flying from Stavanger. On 24 March an Ar 234 reconnoitred the east coast of Scotland and down to Middlesbrough, 'probably for the benefit of U-boats' in a British assessment. On the 25th, U-boat Command reported that aircraft from Norway had counted 21 vessels proceeding independently between Berwick and Hartlepool.

Throughout the Ar 234's brief service with the *Aufklärer*, Burg seems to have been the principal conversion and training base for the aircraft. Indeed, several of the machines there carried the markings of operational *Staffeln*. Oberleutnant Walter Carlein was introduced to the Arado jet there as early as summer 1944; Leutnant Hellmut Hetz flew 9V+GH from Burg on 30 January 1945; Oberfeldwebel Emil Jackstadt of 1.(F)/123

Oberleutnant Fritz Worschech's 4U+EH suffered engine failure on 31 March 1945 and was wrecked in a forced landing at Bispingen. Worschech was only slightly hurt on this occasion, but he would be shot down and killed by Spitfire XIVs from No 350 (Belgian) Sqn on 3 May (*EN Archive*) had logged five flights in four Ar 234s with 1.(F)/100 markings (T5+AH, T5+FH, T5+GH and T5+OH) between 20 January and 8 February 1945; Leutnant Josef Gibitz converted to the Ar 234 in Burg during February 1945, before joining 1.(F)/100 in Lechfeld; and Leutnant Helmut Reinert of 1.(F)/22 and Oberfeldwebel Karl Nitschke of 1.(F)/100 flew from there in T5+BH in early April 1945, their programme including trial photographic runs over Germany.

Allied bombing wrecked Burg on 10 April, and by the following evening US Army troops were just ten kilometres away. On the evening of the 12th, Nitschke took off from the Autobahn south of the aerodrome in Wk-Nr 140609 and headed for Großenhain, before continuing to Lechfeld on the 14th. When Reinert attempted to take off in Wk-Nr 140594 from the same Autobahn on the morning of 13 April, a burst tyre caused the jet to crash, leaving the pilot hospitalised.

Oberleutnant Heinz Schelbert of 1.(F)/33 ferried an Ar 234 to Lechfeld for 1.(F)/100 that same day, this unit having been declared ready for operations at Unterschlauersbach on 1 April. The *Staffel's* orders on the 1st were road reconnaissance in area Alsfeld–Ulrichstein–Fulda–Hersfeld, and establishing the whereabouts of tank concentrations and troop movements in the area bounded by Aschaffenburg–Mannheim–Hockenheim–Mosbach–Buchen–Miltenberg–Wintersbach–Aschaffenburg.

Luftwaffe units were now continually on the move as German-held territory contracted, and on 2 April 1.(F)/100 was transferred to Lechfeld. On the 3rd, Hauptmann Holert signalled (apparently to Burg) that Feldwebel Gildemeister and Oberfeldwebel Puls were to ferry aircraft to this new base. Despite the upheaval, a 30-minute visual reconnaissance was undertaken that morning of roads, including the Frankfurt–Bensheim Autobahn. The unit apparently mounted another three sorties from Unterschlauersbach that day.

Twenty-four hours earlier, orders were issued to find quarters in Wittmundhafen for *Stab* FAGr. 1. That same afternoon British intelligence identified an aircraft plotted off Rattray Head, Scotland, as an Ar 234 of 1.(F)/1. Early on 4 April, Ar 234 9V+BH took off from Wittmundhafen for Hull and the Humber Estuary, sighting coastal shipping and photographing airfields in Yorkshire and Lincolnshire. From Denmark, the Luftwaffe apprised the *Kriegsmarine* of another sortie from Wittmundhafen that morning. Climbing to 9000 m, 9V+AH had headed for Great Yarmouth and Lowestoft, its coverage limited by a broken camera shutter control. 9V+DH, due to cover Ipswich and Harwich, was recalled when its fuel transfer pump failed, while a further Arado encountered thick cloud at 4000 m and was unable to fulfil its task.

Two days later *Stab* FAGr. 1 and 1.(F)/33 were told of plans to transfer them to Grove and Kaltenkirchen, respectively, leaving a skeleton Ar 234 servicing crew in Wittmundhafen. *Stab* FAGr. 1 duly set off by road on the 7th, and 1.(F)/33 was reported as relocating to Schleswig that day.

Luftwaffe Denmark reported that two Ar 234s attempted evening missions on 6 April. The first was to Ipswich and Harwich, but was aborted with technical trouble, while the second, to Great Yarmouth and Lowestoft, was thwarted by solid cloud. An air raid on Kaltenkirchen on the morning of the 9th slightly damaged two Ar 234s. A third jet flew a two-hour reconnaissance from Schleswig that afternoon, photographing

the Great Yarmouth and Harwich areas for the *Kriegsmarine*. The next day a warning was given to friendly units that an Arado of 1.(F)/1 was due to take off from Stavanger at around 1400 hrs, and this was probably the aircraft plotted off Rattray Head from 1518-1543 hrs.

In Italy, two Ar 234s had staged through Lonate on 1 April – Sommer arrived (from Udine) in T9+EH, followed by Gniesmer shortly thereafter in T9+DH (from Osoppo). They left, heading west, at 0914 hrs and 0719 hrs, respectively. Sommer was in the air for more than two hours, covering Corsican airfields, as well as Cecina and Cesena on the mainland. According to the *Kriegsmarine*, the principal harbours in Italy and southern France were photographed. An anti-aircraft unit in Pisa sighted an Arado, estimating its speed at 500 mph, and that day's Allied photo-reconnaissance coverage of Udine revealed the presence of an Ar 234.

A 1.(F)/100 machine photographed Tauberbischofsheim late on the afternoon of 4 April, and the next day one achieved partial cover of roads in the area Wertheim–Miltenberg–Mannheim–Karlsruhe–Heilbronn–Bad Mergentheim. That evening an element of the *Staffel* was in München-Riem, although a signal the following afternoon still placed the unit in Lechfeld.

Over Italy, the 79th FG reported three sightings of 'possible Me 262s' in the Udine area, one allegedly making a pass at them, and on the 5th, according to the RAF, 'An enemy jet-propelled aircraft was seen over our bases this morning. Radar plots gave a height of 35,000 ft and a speed of 400 mph. After a good look round, it moved north toward Venice.' During the morning, Lt Becky of the USAAF's 12th Photo Reconnaissance Squadron (PRS) reported 'Probable J/P [jet-propelled] E/A seen in area south of Bologna, finally heading north and disappearing north of Bologna at 30,000 ft.' Over Lake Comacchio, a USAAF F-5 Lightning pilot claimed a jet had attacked, only to be 'driven off by friendly flak', while a Spitfire reported an Me 262 over Venice. Campoformido was raided by B-24s that

Seen at Grove, in Denmark, 8H+HH (Wk-Nr 140466) belonged to 1.(F)/33. Originally based in Wittmundhafen, this unit undertook coverage of harbours, shipping lanes and airfields in southeast England from March 1945 (*EN Archive*)

same day, dropping an estimated 15,000 fragmentation bombs, but none of the jets was damaged.

Radio traffic suggested that 1.(F)/123 had reconnoitred Almelo, Rheine and Quackenbrück early on 4 April. The following evening, *Stab* FAGr. 123 reported completion of its transfer to Lechfeld, and that 1. *Staffel* was in Reinsehlen. That same afternoon, however, Reinsehlen's Naval Liaison Officer contacted his superiors and asked what he should do if Allied forces approached the airfield, adding that, 'Further transfer eastwards of the *Aufklärer* not to be expected.' A visual reconnaissance was flown that day, the pilot reporting traffic near Rheine, although neither that airfield nor Hopsten was occupied (the Tempest Vs of No 122 Wing RAF would move in within the week, however).

The following morning (6 April) 1.(F)/123 was in the process of transferring to Lübeck-Blankensee when its transport echelon was strafed en route, leaving one dead, five wounded and 'heavy material damage', including the loss of Muffey's logbooks. On the 7th, 1.(F)/123 operated from its new base, the morning sortie covering the Weser from Nienburg to Hameln, the canal between Minden and Rheine and the Dortmund–Ems Canal. The afternoon flight took in Zutphen, Arnhem, Dinslaken and Minden.

Also on the 7th, 1.(F)/100 covered the road from Crailsheim to Schwäbisch Hall and found the former's bridge intact, but had no success finding the 6. SS-Mountain Division, believed to be somewhere in the Bad Orb area. In fact, the US Army had captured the division's survivors after fighting the previous weekend. The next morning, an Ar 234 was in the air for 50 minutes, covering roads and airfields in southern Germany, including the Crailsheim area. Among the pilots aloft were Leutnant Zeeb, Hauptmann Holert and Feldwebel Lippmann (T5+IH). Crailsheim saw intense fighting from 7–11 April, when elements of the US Army's 10th Armored Division and supporting infantry found themselves cut off and had to be supplied by air before they could withdraw.

München-Riem, seen here post-war, was one of 1.(F)/100's bases in April 1945. Between the Ju 88 and Fw 190 in the foreground can be seen the rear fuselage of an Ar 234, possibly 1.(F)/100's T5+GH (Wk-Nr 140338) (*EN Archive*)

Allied photo-reconnaissance on 9 April noted six Ar 234s at Lechfeld and one at Riem. Like jet bases all across Germany, Lechfeld was bombed that day and two of 1.(F)/100's Arados were destroyed, one man of the technical echelon was killed and another seriously wounded. Nevertheless, a single Ar 234 was overheard at 0830 hrs covering the Crailsheim–Illshofen–Giebelstadt area. That evening, the unit reported its strength as 13 pilots (12 operational) and seven aircraft (five serviceable) – one of the unserviceable machines was T5+IH. By the evening of the 12th strength had fallen to only five aircraft (all serviceable).

Oberleutnant Radau of 1.(F)/123 sortied on the 8th, and was able to carry out part of the day's task over conquered or threatened areas of northwest Germany – he flew between 8000 and 8500 m, relying entirely on his cameras. Oberleutant Krüpe, too, flew a purely photographic sortie, covering Celle airfield, Hannover, Hildesheim, Holzminden and Hameln from 8000 m. Rough interpretation of the photographs yielded a lengthy report that evening – several destroyed bridges were noted, along with traffic movements, artillery positions, 800 rail wagons in the station at Minden, artillery spotter aeroplanes on landing grounds and much else.

The next day (9 April) the *Staffel* reported having eight jets (four serviceable), and a deciphered signal revealed that Wk-Nr 140153 was at Lübeck-Blankensee. Radio monitoring also indicated a possible operation by the unit in the Bremen area at around 1745 hrs. According to British intelligence, three of 1.(F)/123's Arados carried out reconnaissance of the areas Bremen–Osnabrück–Paderborn–Kassel–Mühlhausen–Hannover on the 10th.

Gniesmer (T9+DH) arrived in Lonate from Udine at 1015 hrs on the 8th, and did not leave until the following afternoon. His assignment was described as 'south east', suggesting a flight down the Italian Peninsula. Allied reconnaissance spotted the Arado during its stopover, and Gniesmer found it necessary to evade intruding Spitfires when landing back at Campoformido. Sommer, meanwhile, attempted to photograph the western section of the frontline, but he had to abort the flight with engine trouble. The final Allied offensive in Italy opened on 9 April and, as Sommer recalled it, Gniesmer undertook coverage of Forlí on the 10th, when again the Allies photographed an Ar 234 on the ground at Campoformido.

Sommer apparently photographed Taranto, Brindisi and Bari on the 11th, while Gniesmer's final visit to Lonate saw him landing at 0725 hrs and departing at 1110 hrs, flying his usual T9+DH. He was due to cover the frontline between Bologna and Ancona, before returning to Udine. USAAF pilots sighted his machine east of Verona, stating an 'Ar 234 made [an] ineffective pass at bomber SW Bologna, destroyed by escort'.

2Lt Benjamin W Hall III of the Mustang-equipped 52nd FG and his wingman, 2Lt Cooper, were at 20,000 ft when they spotted an aircraft two miles away at a similar altitude. On seeing the fighters, it veered north, although Hall closed to within about 800 yards dead astern and opened fire, hitting the Arado's port nacelle. It took no evasive action, and the American pilots pursued the Ar 234 at full boost but were unable to gain until it began to lose power. Despite difficulty holding position in the

Kommando Sommer's Leutnant Günther Gniesmer was shot down by 2Lts Hall and Cooper of the 52nd FG on 11 April 1945. The wreck of Gniesmer's T9+DH (Wk-Nr 140142) was examined by Allied Field Intelligence soon after, despite orders to local German units to destroy it without fail (*NB Collection*)

jet wash, Hall hit the Arado's tail, fuselage and left wing, then a ball of flame erupted from the port engine and it entered a gentle dive. Cooper then saw strikes on the wings and fuselage and reported that his adversary crashed before the pilot could escape. Sommer, however, said that Gniesmer bailed out and was seriously injured when he struck the aircraft's tail. Landing behind German lines, he died in a Ferrara military hospital on the 13th. Born in Buenos Aires, Leutnant Günther Gniesmer was 22 years old.

The Arado had come down on flat, open ground about 16 km northwest of Alfonsine, and on 12 April a flak unit asked to be notified of the whereabouts of 'One Arado 234, T9+EH overdue, Pilot Lt. Gniesmer. Task from area Milan to front line area Bologna–Ancona.' Although the code is misstated, the message suggests either that the Ar 234's wreckage was not found right away or that word of its discovery had not got back from the frontline. Meanwhile, information had come in from the Wehrmacht's 362nd *Infanterie-Division* that a German aircraft had crashed near Bastia (four kilometres southeast of Argenta) the previous day, and a battalion in the area was told the machine must be 'destroyed without fail, as it is a new type'.

On the evening of 12 April, 1.(F)/123's strength was nine aircraft (three serviceable) and ten pilots (eight operational). On the 13th, Luftwaffe Denmark had proposed to *Luftflotte Reich* that 'owing to the cessation of North Sea recce by 1.(F)/33 as result of fuel situation', security reconnaissance over the North Sea should be continued from Copenhagen by five Bv 138s of 3./SAGr. 126. The following afternoon a Mosquito obtained full coverage of Schleswig-Land, including '1 Ar.234 on W. end of ENE/WSW runway' – the first time that a jet had been spotted on this aerodrome.

Radio traffic indicated at least one morning and two afternoon jet reconnaissance operations over northwest Germany on the 14th. The next morning, an Ar 234 taking off from Kaltenkirchen was downed by Tempest Vs from No 56 Sqn (Flt Lts Neil Cox and Jim McCairns), and there was radio traffic from a jet 'of possibly 1.(F)/123' in the Parchim area that evening.

During the afternoon of the 14th, 1.(F)/100 reconnoitred crossings of the River Main. Two days later, the unit reported Wk-Nr 140611 as newly allocated, and Hauptmann Holert signalled Großenhain asking after both its and Wk-Nr 140612's whereabouts. Oberleutnant Heinz Schelbert and Oberfeldwebel Dahlenburg were supposed to be flying them to Lechfeld, and the former did finally arrive. Dahlenburg, however, had left Großenhain on 14 April, only to turn back and crash land. Schelbert subsequently flew two sorties from Riem.

In Italy, the second phase of a British amphibious assault across Lake Comacchio had begun on 13 April – this may have been when Sommer photographed amphibious craft sailing north along the coast and entering a lagoon. OKL was asked to allocate two Ar 234B-2s immediately 'for maintaining and carrying out urgent operational tasks', perhaps because of the *Kommando's* second loss – Sommer wrote off T9+EH in a belly landing at Campoformido, although he could not remember the exact date. This Arado had a history of hydraulics problems and the main wheels would not come down. To make matters worse, Sommer was caught in a severe crosswind shortly before he force-landed.

No replacements arrived, and Sommer carried on with T9+FH. Nevertheless, two Ar 234s were reported at Udine by Allied reconnaissance on the 15th. Two days later, a 12th PRS pilot saw a vapour trail heading west over Lake Comacchio at about 10,000 m, and a 'possible jet' was reported east of Bologna. On 18 April only one Ar 234 showed up in reconnaissance photographs of Udine, and Allied Field Intelligence reported on the wreck of Gniesmer's aircraft, noting bullet damage from astern and dead level, and that an engine had apparently been on fire in the air. Their impression that the pilot had force-landed was bolstered by finding one torn-off engine 100 m from the rest of the machine. The wreckage appeared to have been set on fire by retreating German troops and its Rb 75/30 cameras were burnt out. The *Werk Nummer* 140142, was painted on the fin and 'Squadron markings were ?? plus D(?)H in large black letters, while a large black D was painted, outboard on the undersurfaces of the wing.'

Over Wertingen, in Bavaria, on 18 April, the P-47s from the 356th FG were escorting B-26s when 'a bogie was called in high at twelve o'clock to us – he was at about 12,000 ft when we first saw him but [he] turned to the left in a shallow dive'. Green Section attacked, although its leader, 1Lt Jack Cornett, broke off after a few bursts, apparently unsure his target was hostile. 1Lt Leon Oliver, in no such doubt, closed in and opened fire, seeing strikes on the port wing, engine nacelle and fuselage. He smelt 'the odour of burning low-grade fuel' as the port jet started to smoke and he kept firing. As Oliver pulled past, the jet went into a spin and hit the ground between two houses, which then caught fire, none of the Americans believing the pilot had got out.

Another Ar 234 was shot down that day by Lt Col Dale E Shafer of the P-51-equipped 339th FG southeast of Regensburg. Exploiting a height advantage, he was able to obtain strikes that resulted in the jet's cockpit

Lt Col Dale E Shafer, commanding officer of the 339th FG's 503rd FS, claimed an Ar 234 destroyed at 1225 hrs on 18 April southeast of Regensburg while at the controls of his assigned P-51D. The Arado – probably from 1.(F)/100 – was Shafer's seventh, and final, victory of the war (*NARA*)

hatch coming off and, as it entered a dive, the pilot bailing out before Shafer saw the Arado hit the ground and explode.

That morning, 1.(F)/100's Leutnant Beck (T5+IH) had taken off from Riem to reconnoitre roads round Chemnitz but he was unable to complete his mission for reasons unknown. The *Staffel's* Oberfeldwebel Willi Windhövel died the following day, reportedly at Dietfurt – a location not close to either USAAF claim.

An Arado of 1.(F)/1 was due up from Stavanger on 19 April, British intelligence understanding it to be searching for an invasion force supposedly headed for Scandinavia. On the 21st the *General der Aufklärungsflieger* announced that 1.(F)/5 was being disbanded, with 1.(F)/33 taking over the 'entire task' of reconnaissance for U-boat operations. *Einsatzkommando* 1.(F)/5 would therefore be subsumed into 1.(F)/33. *Stab* FAGr. 123 announced its own disbandment on 17 April, but signals traffic indicated two brief sorties by 1. *Staffel* on the 19th, and early the next day a 'possible jet recce' was overheard in the northern sector.

On 21 April, Rechlin was told that 1.(F)/123 would collect Wk-Nr 140105, and on the 25th the RAF's summary of coverage of North German airfields noted that 'Arado 234 Jet Aircraft are still present at LUEBECK/BLANKENSEE, with a probable Ar. 234 visible at HOHN for the first time.' The latter had been seen on the morning of 24 April under tow at one end of the east/west runway, and Muffey recalled how '[at the] end of April we reached our last resort at Hohn, where we just waited for the big turn of fate'.

A machine from 1.(F)/100 was up on the 21st, providing photographic coverage of an area between Stuttgart and Nuremberg. By then its strength had sunk to five aircraft (three serviceable) and 13 pilots (12 operational). The next day's reconnaissance of roads between Amberg, Bayreuth, Bamberg and Roth was fruitless as the Ar 234 crashed into a wood and Leutnant Josef Gibitz sustained multiple injuries. Waking in American captivity after spending three weeks unconscious, he no longer knew whether he had been shot down or suffered a malfunction, only that one engine had been on fire.

On 22 April the American 12th Armored Division seized an intact bridge over the Danube at Dillingen, taking three more the next day. This was the context for Oberfeldwebel Karl Nitschke's first war flight – visual reconnaissance of the crossings between Ulm and Ingolstadt. Flying T5+BH, he took off from Lechfeld on the afternoon of the 24th and landed at Riem. The Allies intercepted a report of this flight's results, plus another that morning covering roads and airfields around Erlangen, Nürnberg and Herzogenaurach. Although *Luftflotte* 6 had given 1.(F)/100's location as Lechfeld on 21 April, evidently the *Staffel* was still using two airfields. This is confirmed by a signal sent early on the 25th advising that Feldwebel Lippmann had taken off in T5+EH to carry out 'Task B', while 'Task A' would be flown from Riem. That same day Nitschke used T5+JH (or T5+IH) for a photo-reconnaissance of Regensburg and Amberg.

Oberleutnant Walter Carlein, who flew with 1.(F)/100, recalled Hauptmann Holert being shot down over Augsburg shortly after take-off at around this time, and that a Hauptmann Oech apparently stood in for about a week before Carlein himself became *Staffelführer*. Augsburg

is 20 km north of Lechfeld, where the *Staffel* had arrived in early April. Holert's name appears in a signal of the 16th, and he was not one of the two pilots known to have been lost on 18 April (as noted earlier in this chapter), although the decrypted report on the day's operations is incomplete. Leutnant Gibitz recalled attending Holert's wake in Königsbrunn (eight kilometres from Lechfeld) shortly before his own crash on the 22nd, and that the Hauptmann had been shot down near Ingolstadt.

On 25 April P-51s of the 479th FG were at 24,000 ft near Traunstein when 2Lt Hilton O Thompson (who had previously claimed an Me 262 shot down on 7 April) spotted an enemy jet and climbed towards it. The hostile turned to the southeast and the American pilot was able to close to 700 yards, where, with the aid of his K-14 gyro gunsight, he scored hits on its port engine. Drawing nearer, Thompson saw strikes on the port fuselage and pieces flying off. 2Lt Harold B Stotts also achieved hits, the Ar 234 spiralling down until the pilot bailed out. Thompson believed his victim had crashed near Berchtesgaden, about 35 km from the initial encounter, and the wreckage of T5+BH (Wk-Nr 140611) was later found in woods there. This aircraft proved to be the Eighth Air Force's last aerial victory of the war.

American troops had reached the River Lech by the evening of 27 April, the Augsburg–Lechfeld area itself was in their hands by the following evening and Munich was taken on the 30th. Although 1.(F)/100 had been assigned missions to Bavarian targets on the 29th, it is not known whether any were actually flown.

In Italy, the US troops had broken into the Po Valley and the British Eighth Army had passed through the Argenta Gap. Allied forces entered Bologna on 21 April and the Americans reached the River Po itself three days later. Luftwaffe operations were drawing to a close, with J2 stocks rapidly depleting as aviation fuel was doled out for retreating vehicles.

The remains of T5+BH (Wk-Nr 140611) of 1.(F)/100 was photographed where the aircraft crashed at Berchtesgaden on 25 April 1945 after being attacked by 2Lts Hilton O Thompson and Harold B Stotts of the 434th FS/479th FG. It had the unfortunate distinction of being the last German aircraft shot down by the Eighth Air Force (*Linda Korienek/James V. Crow Collection*)

There were jet sightings over Bologna, Ravenna and Venice on 20 April, and a P-51 chased an Ar 234 over Padua. After one such incident a Luftwaffe listening unit passed Oberleutnant Sommer a transcript of Mustang pilots complaining that 'He's too bloody fast!' On the 22nd, Sommer (T9+FH) flew a reconnaissance of the Po Valley, and the next day an Ar 234 was seen under tow to its take-off point at Campoformido. His task for the 24th was battle and tactical reconnaissance on the German Fourteenth Army's front over Viadana–Reggio Emilia–Bologna–Bergantino, and the morning sortie brought multiple sightings by Allied airmen;

'Possible jet plane heading north from Ferrara at approx. 25,000 ft.'

'U/i [unidentified] a/c seen making trails at about 25,000 ft Mantua. Pilot thought u/i a/c was travelling unusually fast.'

'Pilot noticed vapour trails at 30,000 ft heading from L. Comacchio for Mantua. At Mantua a/c made a circle and headed back to Lake Commacchio then to Udine.'

The last time Allied photo-reconnaissance reported an Ar 234 at Udine was on 25 April, with the RAF also noting a possible jet over the front, and sightings by Spitfires near Venice and of one going north in the Ostiglia–Udine area. A USAAF pilot, meanwhile, reported 'one Me 262' over Quistello.

Sommer related how Oberfeldwebel Arnold left Campoformido on the 28th in the surviving Ar 234 with orders to make for Bolzano or Riem, depending on the weather. In a climate where supposed deserters faced summary execution, Sommer had prudently secured written orders to withdraw to Bolzano and set off with his ground echelon over the mountain roads. In an exchange of fire with partisans the *Kommando*'s papers, including his own logbooks and diaries, were lost in a trailer that went over a precipice – their aerial photos had been destroyed before departure.

The British Second Army had crossed the Elbe at Lauenburg on 29 April. Two days later, five reconnaissance aircraft from 14.*Fliegerdivision* sortied before 1400 hrs, covering the bridgehead and the Stade–Boizenburg sector. The only reported results from these operations mentioned Allied tanks. On 2 May there was radio evidence of two morning operations in the Stade–Hamburg area, one at midday west of Kiel and an evening sortie over Lauenburg. The British reached Travemünde (100 km by road from Lauenburg) that day, cutting off the jet bases in Schleswig-Holstein and Denmark.

On the afternoon of the 3rd, the Allies overheard traffic from a 'possible jet recce west and north west of Hamburg' (the city surrendered that same day). Plt Off Des Watkins of No 350 (Belgian) Sqn was leading Pink Section's four Spitfire XIVs on armed reconnaissance when, at about 1310 hrs, he spotted a jet in the circuit at Hohn, identifying it as an Ar 234. The Spitfires dived, Watkins closing to 50 yards before opening fire and hitting the Arado's wings and fuselage, leaving it smoking. Flt Lt Patrick Bangerter later noted in his combat report;

'I followed after Pink 1 and chased E/A as it was crossing aerodrome boundary at 200 ft approximately. E/A turned port with flaps and u/c down. I followed and fired cannon with a 5° angle deflection, and obtained strikes on port wing root and port engine, saw flames.'

Flt Sgt André Kicq and Flg Off Albert Van Eckhoud attacked together and saw strikes, before breaking away when they began to overshoot. Kicq reported, 'Five seconds later E/A flipped on its back, port mainplane fell off, and E/A struck the ground in a ball of fire.' The Arado's pilot, 23-year-old Oberleutnant Fritz Worschech, did not survive his aircraft's disintegration and is buried at Fahrdorf, near Schleswig.

A reconnaissance Spitfire flew over Leck early on 3 May, its photographs revealing one Ar 234 in the northern dispersal, two in the 'north remote dispersal' and three more in the southwest corner of the airfield. The same sortie found a 'probable' Ar 234 at Schleswig. *Luftflotte* 6 recorded 1.(F)/100's location as Hörsching, in Austria, and Oberfeldwebel Nitschke had evacuated T9+NL (a partially equipped Ar 234 nightfighter) there from Riem on 29 April, before continuing to Prague-Ruzyne and then Zatec. Oberleutnant Carlein recounted that his last act as *Staffelführer* was to disband 1.(F)/100 on the Czech/Bavarian border on 8 or 9 May before making his way home. Oberleutnant Schelbert and four other officers from the *Staffel* were drafted into a ground unit at Zeltweg, but Germany capitulated before they saw action.

When German forces in northwest Germany and Denmark surrendered on 4 May, 1.(F)/123 was still at Hohn. Luftwaffe schedules prepared by the unit for the British occupiers give no figures for either aircraft or personnel still with the *Staffel*, although two machines, Wk-Nr 140141 (4U+FH) and 140581, had been evacuated to Stavanger by this time. Götz had

The derelict fuselage of ??+HH, photographed in South Germany after VE Day. The location and markings point to an aircraft of 1.(F)/100, which took over a T5+HH (Wk-Nr 140315) on 15 January 1945 (*EN Archive*)

The former 8H+DH (Wk-Nr 140476) of 1.(F)/33 was taken over and tested by the RAF after it was captured at Grove (*EN Archive*)

told his pilots they could fly home, but his own machine's landing gear collapsed, so he was stranded. Werner Muffey remembered how 'the last of all our Ar 234s were blown up one morning after 9 May at Hohn airfield, amongst them my T9+KH'. A report to OKL on 22 May 1945 still listed Hauptmann Horst Götz as the *Staffel's* CO.

In Campoformido, Allied Field Intelligence found;

'Ar 234. No. 234-292. No. on fin: 140344.

'Condition: Burnt and demolished.

'Engines: Jet units missing.

'Marking: ? (cross) H black.

'Wing of Ar 234. Serial No. 234-292. Wk. Nr. 408010.'

The missing engines were found in a building in Udine, one having caught fire and the other suffering from 'superficial damage caused by a crash and mishandling'. It appeared that looters had already got to both. Learning of these discoveries in 1989, Erich Sommer wrote, 'This means that instead of blowing them up as I had directed, my men just left them there. It could have cost me my head.' Sommer and Heinz Arnold met again in a post-war internment camp, Arnold explaining that he had landed his Arado in Holzkirchen, Bavaria, and blown it up there the next day.

In Stavanger on 4 May, Leutnant Hetz had been allowed to fly (in 9V+BH) for the first time since his crash in March. On the 6th, according to a list drawn up for the Allies, the jet units in Denmark were 1.(F)/33 (Ar 234 and Ju 188 – 219 personnel, including eight aircrew), 1.(F)/5 (Ar 234 – 95 personnel) and *Stab* FAGr. 1 (Ar 234 – 15 personnel, including two aircrew). All were said to be at Grove, although another document placed *Einsatzkommando* FAGr. 1 at Stavanger on 18 May. The final British Air Forces of Occupation report on the dissolution of the Luftwaffe lists ten Ar 234s in British-occupied Germany, six in Denmark and seven in Norway.

9V+CH (Wk-Nr 140493) of 1.(F)/1 is refuelled by RAF personnel after it was captured in Stavanger, Norway (*EN Archive*)

CHAPTER FIVE

REMAGEN AND RETREAT

From late February 1945, the US First and Ninth Armies attacked along the River Roer, their main thrust being directed at the town of Jülich. As part of German efforts to repel the Americans, on the morning of the 25th III./KG 76 attacked concentrations of troops of the Ninth Army near to the town of Linnich, 12 km to the north of Jülich. Eighteen Ar 234s bombed US troop positions, scoring hits on roads and bridges across the Roer. Two Arados were in turn lost that day. Unteroffizier Arnold Przetak of 8. *Staffel* is believed to have been shot down in Wk-Nr 140456 (F1+AS), and he crashed near Bohmte, between Achmer airfield and the Dümmer See. It is possible his assailants may have been P-51 pilots 1Lt Richard White and 2Lt Eugene Murphy of the 364th FG. Oberleutnant Kolm, *Staffelkapitän* of 8./KG 76, bailed out near Achmer, having also been claimed by fighters.

As February gave way to March, there was a change in the leadership of III./KG 76 when Major Bätcher handed over command of the *Gruppe* to Major Franz Zauner, an Austrian and a recipient of the Knight's Cross. Zauner had flown more than 200 missions. On the Eastern Front, he and the crew of his Ju 88 had claimed the destruction of eight trains, 110 lorries, five tanks and six aircraft on the ground. Zauner's subsequent record in the Mediterranean was also impressive, where, as leader of III./KG 54, he flew anti-shipping operations, before being transferred to northwest Europe to fly against England and over France from mid-1944.

The *Gruppenkommandeur* of III./KG 76, Major Hansgeorg Bätcher, second from right, is seen in conversation with Major i.G. Rammig, Operations Officer of II. *Jagdkorps*, at far left, and Generalmajor Karl-Eduard Wilke, commander of II. *Jagdkorps*, probably at Achmer in late February 1945. At far right is Hauptmann Diether Lukesch, and visible between Rammig and Wilke is probably Major Franz Zauner, Bätcher's successor. This photograph may have been taken at the time of the change in command (*EN Archive*)

Meanwhile, II./KG 76 was still completing its conversion training to the Ar 234, with elements at Burg and Alt-Lönnewitz. By 25 February most of 6. *Staffel* was ready for combat, the unit's 16 Arados under Hauptmann Gerhard Morich – another Knight's Cross-holder and formerly *Staffelkapitän* of 4./KG 4 – having relocated to Hesepe, just north of Achmer, from where it was to conduct operations.

US forces were closing on the Rhine by early March, having taken Mönchengladbach on the 1st. The following day, 22 Ar 234s from KG 76, including two aircraft from the *Geschwaderstab* which made its operational debut that day, struck at American armour and troop columns between Mönchengladbach, Jülich and Düren, as well as further west at Maastricht. For this mission, the jets enjoyed the benefit of fighter cover from Bf 109s of II., III. and IV./JG 27, which patrolled Achmer between 0725 and 0830 hrs, before heading off to make low-level attacks on enemy forces. However, as the jet bombers headed towards their targets, at least one was spotted near Nijmegen by Flt Sgt H Kelly, who was flying a Spitfire XIV of No 41 Sqn from Volkel. He reported;

'I immediately gave chase, instructing my No. 2 to slow down and drop his jet tank, being unable to do so myself due to the high speed. The enemy aircraft turned slightly to Starboard and continued towards the North East, weaving slightly from time to time. I kept out of the enemy pilot's view by keeping under his tailplane and slowly overhauled him at an IAS of 340 mph at 8/9,000 ft. I closed to 100 yards or less, firing with 5 MG and cannon whilst still overtaking. I saw strikes on the Port wing, Port jet engine and fuselage. Enemy aircraft immediately emitted dense clouds of brownish black smoke, possibly jet exhaust. I continued firing and saw flashes in the smoke, breaking away at extremely close range and being hit in the Port radiator by debris. I next saw enemy aircraft going down in a wide spiral to Starboard with white smoke or vapour pouring from holes all along the Port wing, and dark smoke from the fuselage.

'I could then see the long nose of the aircraft and the straight tapered wings with rounded tips and identified enemy aircraft as an Arado 234. A large piece of enemy aircraft suddenly flew off, and one person bailed out, parachute opening. Enemy aircraft steepened its dive and crashed somewhere near Enschede, being completely destroyed by explosion. Some fire from the ground was seen at this time.'

This was most likely the aircraft of Oberleutnant Sütterlin of 9./KG 76, who bailed out safely.

Elsewhere, Tempest Vs of No 222 Sqn clashed with the Bf 109s of IV./JG 27 covering Achmer. A large aerial engagement broke out, during which Flt Lt L McAuliffe went after a pair of Ar 234s he spotted near Lingen. They soon out-paced him. Flt Lt G W Varley made an understandable initial misinterpretation also in the Lingen area;

'I immediately saw crossing our formation from starboard to port what appeared to be a Horsa glider, and I realised this was the new Arado jet plane. I dived and turned to port and closed to 1,000 yds and fired a 1 second burst 10 degrees deflection, and looking down and around, saw another jet plane flying below in the other direction. I closed to 200 yds and fired a 2 second burst dead astern, and a huge explosion with red flame occurred. When enemy aircraft blew up, Yellow 1 yelled "break port".'

Varley then found himself in the midst of around 12 Bf 109s, and he was able to claim one destroyed, along with the Arado, before escaping. 'His' Ar 234 may well have been the aircraft flown by Leutnant Eberhard Rögele of 9./KG 76, who crashed at Ibbenbüren.

On 3 March the Americans reached the Rhine at Neuss, and for the next few days inclement weather halted Ar 234 bombing operations. It was during this respite that US forces approached the west bank of the Rhine at Remagen, to the south of Bonn, where they found the Ludendorff railway bridge to be still intact with Wehrmacht troops retreating across it. Alarm bells rang throughout the regional German commands, and on the morning of the 9th *Gefechtsverband Kowalewski*, the tactical command led by Oberstleutnant Kowalewski that directed operations by 6., 8. and 9./KG 76 and the Me 262s of I. and II./KG 51, issued a clear instruction;

'It is important that the enemy's traffic across the river near Remagen should be impeded with all means by destroying the bridges, exploiting any possible weather situation.'

At around the same time the Supreme Allied Commander, Gen Dwight Eisenhower, told Gen Omar Bradley, commander of the US 12th Army Group, 'Hold on to it, Brad. Get across with whatever you need – but make certain you hold that bridgehead.' The circumstances were set for what would become a key target for the Ar 234s of KG 76 over the coming weeks. *Gefechtsverband Kowalewski* ordered that the jet bomber units were to mount continual attacks on the bridge at Remagen with all available strength, as well as against Erpel and along the Remagen–Ahrweiler valley road running from the west.

By this stage, KG 76's standard tactic had become the *Gleitangriff* from 4000 to 2000 m, with most missions involving either SC 500 bombs or AB 500 *Abwurfbehälter* loaded with SD 15 fragmentation bombs, although on occasion 250 kg bombs were also used.

During the early afternoon of 9 March three Ar 234s from III./KG 76 were each loaded with a 250 kg bomb and sent to attack Remagen under *Egon* navigational guidance. Two of the three jets dropped their bombs over the bridge, but the third, flown by Oberfeldwebel Friedrich Bruchlos of 8. *Staffel*, drew fire from American anti-aircraft guns. Flying Wk-Nr 140589 F1+AS, he attempted to release his bomb but his aircraft was seen subsequently by witnesses on the ground around 14 km southeast of Remagen trailing smoke and being fired at by Allied fighters. Bruchlos was killed when he crashed in a valley between Fockenbach and Neuwied.

Remagen became a focal point for the Luftwaffe, and in addition to Ar 234s and Me 262s, it deployed Ju 87s from NSGs 1 and 2 and Fw 190s from NSG 20, III./JG 2 and II./KG 200 in determined attacks that also included using 500 and 1000 kg HE bombs. *Reichsmarschall* Göring even called for volunteers to carry out self-sacrificial operations against the bridge.

Poor weather and persistent technical problems plagued the Ar 234s' attempts to hit the bridge. Indeed, on 11 March a planned mission by III./KG 76 was called off because of low cloud and poor visibility. Notwithstanding this, *Gefechtsverband Kowalewski* pressed for 'destructive attacks' using heavy bombs. The following day it is believed that four Ar 234s from the *Geschwaderstab* and 6./KG 76 carried out a rare horizontal attack from 8000 m under *Egon* navigation. A total of 14 aircraft from

Oberfeldwebel Erich Bäumler of 6./KG 76 was a very experienced bomber pilot and instructor who flew several missions in the Ar 234. He was shot down on 14 March 1945 after being pursued by P-51 pilot 1Lt Robert E Barnhart of the 356th FG (*Roger Gaemperle*)

III./KG 76 undertook two missions that day, with heavy SC 1000 bombs included among the ordnance. Effects could not be observed because of the weather and one jet returned with its bomb still attached, the pilot having failed to locate the bridge. Indeed, the challenges faced by the Luftwaffe at Remagen were portrayed in a signal issued by 15.*Fliegerdivision* that day;

'Operations at dawn and during the day could not be carried out because clouds were too low. After the cloud base lifted in the late afternoon in the battle area, ops at dusk were similarly impossible.'

The next morning (12th), following a meteorological reconnaissance sortie over the bridge area by a single Ar 234 from III./KG 76, 11 Arados from the *Gruppe* carried out a strike at various points during the morning and lasting until 1400 hrs, again apparently using *Egon* guidance. It seems the Ar 234s attacked in pairs from around 5000 m, dropping one 1000 kg Trialen bomb, five SC 500 bombs and three AB 500s loaded with SD 10 fragmentation bombs, but again effects could not be ascertained. Later in the day, 12 Ar 234s of III. *Gruppe* again attacked the bridge, although on this occasion Unteroffizier Zwiener was forced to bail out near Wesendorf. This attack was followed by another effort involving five jets against the road between Mergentheim and Bonn. They dropped four 1000 kg bombs and a single AB 500 loaded with SD 15 fragmentation bombs. Finally, towards dusk, two Ar 234s flew an armed reconnaissance over the bridgehead before releasing AB 500/SD 15s in a glide attack over Oberwinter, eight kilometres to the north along the Rhine. One jet was posted missing, possibly as a result of being engaged by P-51s.

In clearer skies on the 14th, III. *Gruppe* and 6./KG 76 despatched 19 Ar 234s in total between 1213 and 1528 hrs. This mission involved many challenges, and at least one aircraft had to abort as a result of technical issues. Within minutes of leaving the ground, the remaining jets were intercepted by Allied fighters. The *Kampfflieger* doggedly climbed into the air, through the enemy, and flew on, using their superior speed to literally out-pace their attackers. The jets passed over the Laacher-See and then headed north towards the Rhine, approaching Remagen in *Ketten* (two-aircraft elements) from the south. Over the target, the jets bombed an American pontoon bridge and roads on the bank close by with eight SC 500s and two 1000 kg bombs.

After having dropped his SC 500 Trialen bomb onto the Ludendorff bridge that afternoon, Oberfeldweber Erich Bäumler of 6./KG 76 made course to Hesepe. However, as he flew back to base he was set upon by what he identified as a group of P-38 Lightnings. In the ensuing attack, one of his Jumo 004s received hits and the aircraft's cockpit glazing disintegrated under fire. Bäumler was a very able airman, with combat experience of flying Ju 88s in Russia with II./KG 3, and he later served as an instructor. Despite his sudden precarious predicament, he thus put to use all of his flying skill to escape the Lightnings by diving into cloud. Although he successfully shook off the P-38s, when he emerged from the clouds in the Bielefeld area, he found that his troubles were far from over.

At that very moment 1Lt Robert Barnhart of the 356th FG was leading a flight of P 51s escorting B-17s returning from a raid to Hildesheim. Having only left the target area ten minutes earlier, he returned to Hildesheim when the call of 'bandits' in the area came over the R/T. Barnhart 'patrolled uneventfully for ten minutes and then headed out'. Then, as he passed near to Bielefeld at around 10,000 ft, he spotted an unidentifiable aircraft off to his right;

1Lt Robert Barnhart of the 356th FG poses with his P-51D *Margie Darling* at Martlesham Heath, Suffolk, shortly after shooting down Oberfeldwebel Erich Bäumler on 14 March 1945. Bäumler had been forced to bail out of his jet bomber after being pursued by Barnhart (*Tom Ivie*)

'Since I could not identify it, and since it was heading directly into Germany all alone, I did a quick 180° turn and pursued it. The chase started at range of approximately 2,500 yards. After 10-15 minutes at full throttle I was unable to close. Due to impending fuel shortage I was about to break off when the plane, apparently unaware of us in pursuit, made a left turn (to the north) and I was able to cut him off. This was in the Hildesheim area. Unable to identify it, I closed until I saw the open jets and German markings. Knowing that I had him cold, I slid under him and came up on his right about thirty feet from him in order to get a good look at the plane. I could not identify it then, but have since recognised it from drawings as an Arado 234. The pilot of the jet looked over at me, immediately jettisoned his canopy, and bailed out.'

As Bäumler attempted to exit his aircraft, dropping between the engine and the wing, he was pushed back by the blasting rush of air and he struck the tailplane. The blow caused him to momentarily lose consciousness, but he recovered just in time to release his parachute. His jet smashed into the ground and exploded and Bäumler landed at Altenhagen, ten kilometres east of Bielefeld, from where farmers took him to a hospital at Rinteln.

6./KG 76's Fahnenjunker-Feldwebel Riemensperger was also attacked during the return flight to Hesepe, the former 6./KG 100 pilot being intercepted by two Tempest Vs possibly flown by Flt Lt L McAuliffe and Flg Off D G C McCleland from No 222 Sqn who were on a sweep from Gilze-Rijen. McAuliffe, who it will be recalled had already encountered the Ar 234 on a previous occasion, spotted such a machine just over a mile away and immediately dived with McCleland towards the ground in pursuit of the German jet. He subsequently reported;

Flt Lt L McAuliffe of Tempest V-equipped No 222 Sqn had two encounters with the Ar 234s of KG 76, the second of which took place on 14 March 1945 when he claimed a shared victory with Flg Off D G C McCleland of the same squadron. It is possible that his victim was Fahnenjunker-Feldwebel Riemensperger of 6./KG 76 (*CT Collection*)

'I fired two short bursts while enemy aircraft was turning to port in evasion at 500 yds. My No. 2 also fired. We were catching enemy aircraft up all the time and as it crossed the airfield perimeter (Quakenbruk [sic]) it suddenly dived to the ground, exploding and catching fire.'

As the Arado headed for the ground McCleland broke away on account of intense accurate light flak that had opened up around the airfield, and he did not observe the impact. The Tempest V pilots shared the claim for an Ar 234 destroyed.

Flg Off D G C McCleland of No 222 Sqn, who, along with Flt Lt McAuliffe, claimed an Ar 234 in a shared victory on 14 March 1945 which may have been the aircraft of Fahnenjunker-Feldwebel Riemensperger of 6./KG 76 lost in the Quakenbrück area (*CT Collection*)

Leutnant Werner Croissant, also from 6./KG 76, was intercepted by Allied fighters as he too headed in the direction of Hesepe – the Ar 234's radio was knocked out by enemy fire. He made an emergency landing at Münster-Handorf and was strafed by Mustangs as he left his aircraft.

'All operations were menaced by Tempests and Mustangs', wrote Hauptmann Morich, *Staffelkapitän* of 6./KG 76. 'Our main problem was taking off and landing when speeds were low. Once in the air, the Arado was usually fast enough to evade interception from piston-engined fighters, except when surprised by diving attacks.' The 14th had indeed been a bad day, with Morich also being attacked by a Tempest V, Leutnant Amann shot down over the Westerwald by a P-47 from the 56th FG and Feldwebel Schulz forced to bail out of his Ar 234 over North Rhine-Westphalia, losing an arm as a result.

The last pilot from the unit to be downed on 14 March was Hauptmann Johannes Hirschberger, who was making his first operational flight in an Ar 234. East of the Rhine, he was chased by a P-51 probably flown by Capt Donald Bryan of the 352nd FG. The veteran ace reported observing an Ar 234 as the A-26 Invader formation he was escorting was crossing the Rhine on its return from a bombing mission. Bryan jettisoned his drop tanks and turned east to go after the jet. Having expended almost all of his ammunition on the Arado, Bryan had hit its left Jumo engine and observed the bomber trailing white smoke. Seconds later it turned over onto its back and dived into the ground, the jet exploding on a wooded hillside east of the Rhine, opposite Remagen.

Elsewhere that same day, two Ar 234s undertook another attack on the southern area of Antwerp docks with SC 500s. Both jets returned safely, with poor visibility over the target area preventing bombing effects from being observed.

6./KG 76 attempted to return to Remagen on 17 March, deploying five Ar 234s in single sorties throughout the afternoon, of which only two made it as far as the target area, where Hauptmann Morich and Feldwebel Wördemann dropped AB 500s with SD 15s on American positions in the bridgehead at Erpel. That same day the Ludendorff bridge finally collapsed, but by the 21st the US Army had laid five pontoons across the river. The Luftwaffe had deployed 372 aircraft against Remagen, with 25 of them lost within a 50 km radius of the town.

Commencing on the night of 17 March, operations by III./KG 76 were once again directed at targets in Belgium, with *Gefechtsverband Kowalewski* issuing orders for the *Gruppe* to attack the port of Antwerp – this mission was subsequently cancelled. On the morning of the 19th, however, 15 Ar 234s bombed railway yards in Brussels, dropping AB 500s and both 500 and 1000 kg bombs. Trains were hit and fires broke out in nearby warehouses. Fahnenjunker-Feldwebel Riemensperger of 6. *Staffel* endured a particularly tough day on 19 March. During the morning, while attempting to bomb a railway line near Charleroi, he was chased by a large formation of Spitfires. That afternoon his Ar 234 was hit by anti-aircraft fire as he attacked tanks near Bad Kreuznach on the Nahe river. Despite fire ravaging the structure of his right undercarriage, Riemensperger made a safe, one-wheel landing at Achmer. Moments after he exited the aircraft it burst into flames.

In the evening, four Ar 234s carrying three AB 500s loaded with SD 15s and one SC 500 went back to Bad Kreuznach, where they attacked tanks and soft-skinned vehicles of the US Third Army in a *Gleitangriff* from 2000 m down to 600 m. Results could not be observed. Such missions became the norm, with the Ar 234s used increasingly as ground-attack aircraft. Indeed, on the 20th, 15 jets operated over Bad Kreuznach, dropping AB 500s carrying SD 10 and SD 15 fragmentation bombs as well as SC 500 Trialen bombs in glide attacks against enemy armour, anti-aircraft gun positions and the local railway station. No Ar 234s were lost.

Armourers hitch a ride on a trailer laden with an SC 500 bomb. Behind can be seen an Ar 234 that already appears to be bombed up and ready for its next sortie. The cockpit entrance hatch is open and a packed parachute lies just behind it (*EN Archive*)

The next day 15 Ar 234s again bombed Bad Kreuznach and the surrounding areas. Hauptmann Morich led a formation of four jets from 6./KG 76 against armoured and transport columns and anti-aircraft gun positions to the northeast of the town. Later on the 21st, III./KG 76 suffered a major blow when, at 1800 hrs, Hauptmann Josef Regler, *Kapitän* of 9. *Staffel*, dived vertically into the ground at Achmer as he returned from a reconnaissance flight to the Dutch coast. It was believed his aircraft had been hit by friendly flak, and that Regler had lost consciousness as his Arado accelerated while attempting to avoid being hit. His place at the head of 9./KG 76 was taken by Oberleutnant Wolf Jäger.

Conditions at all of KG 76's airfields had become very hazardous. Landing was an especially dangerous moment because of the risk of enemy fighter attack as the jets slowed to approach – a situation made all the more likely because of the increasingly luckless attempts to muster timely and adequate fighter cover from the local *Jagdgruppen*.

Additionally, as in the USAAF raids of 21 March against the known jet bases, the Arado pilots were given a taste of their own actions when fragmentation bombs were dropped on Hesepe. Leutnant Werner Croissant of 6. *Staffel* recounted having to take cover in a flak gun position as American fighters made a low-level attack on the airfield using 'frag' bombs. For 30 minutes he watched as the bombs detonated when they hit trees, after which their splinters rained down through the branches. At Achmer the *Gruppenstab* lost 13 Ar 234s on the ground as a result of aerial bombing. After the mission, the Eighth Air Force reported on the effects of the raid;

'H.E. bursts are seen covering practically all of the landing area with the exception of the extreme west end. Many hits are noted on each of the runways, rendering them unserviceable, as well as the taxi tracks leading from the dispersal areas. The Northeast corner of the airfield is blanketed with fragmentation bursts, as is most of the South dispersal area adjacent to the landing ground. H.E. bursts also cover a large part of the South dispersal area. Of the 35 aircraft visible at the time of the attack, at least

20 are probably damaged, mostly by fragmentation bursts. Of the 1,528 H.E. bombs dropped, approximately 900 bursts may be seen on clear photographs.'

Hesepe airfield was rendered inoperable until 1 April following the 21 March attack, by which time a 600-m long runway had been completed – just long enough for an Ar 234 fitted with RATO units to take-off *without* a full load of fuel and weapons.

The final operations in March 1945 were flown on the 29th and 30th. During the evening of the last of these two days, two Arados bombed Allied troops around the town of Dülmen with SC 500s, only 40 km to the west of the *Einsatzstaffel's* old airfield at Handorf, while a third attacked a column of tanks and vehicles near Haltern am See. It is believed other aircraft conducted a reconnaissance of the canals at Dorsten-Datteln and Greven-Riesenbeck, as well as roads in the Korbach and Bad Wildungen areas.

Irrespective of the aforementioned runway repairs, on 1 April, fitted with RATO units, the few remaining Ar 234s of 6./KG 76 – at this stage four aircraft at the most – relocated from Hesepe, via Vörden (where they refuelled) and Reinsehlen, north to Marx, an airfield to the southwest of Wilhelmshaven. However, conditions there were no better than at Hesepe or Achmer. The airfield had been one of those bombed by the Eighth Air Force on 21 March, wrecking much of its infrastructure and facilities and leaving the runways and perimeter tracks badly cratered.

In similar moves, the *Geschwaderstab*, which reported two serviceable Arados, left Burg to transfer to airfields in the Lübeck area, while the bulk of II./KG 76 departed Alt-Lönnewitz for Burg, where it was hoped training could continue for the Ar 234 using a single Me 262. A detachment of personnel from the *Geschwaderstab* remained briefly at Achmer under the *Geschwader Adjutant*, Hauptmann Heinrich Tryba, with a view to ensuring that rare items such as spare turbojets did not fall into enemy hands. Eventually, however, they too were compelled to depart to join the elements of II. *Gruppe* at Burg.

By early April even travelling between Burg and Achmer had become a dangerous proposition. On one occasion the *Kommodore's* car was shot up by an armoured vehicle from an advanced British Army unit on a road between the two locations, forcing Oberstleutnant Robert Kowalewski and his driver to take cover in a ditch until the danger had passed.

Despite such adversities on the ground, in the air, KG 76 continued its bombing operations. On 2 April British forces advancing in vehicles at Emsdetten and Ladbergen were bombed by Ar 234s that dropped AB 500s and SC 250s, while a lone Arado carried out reconnaissance over the Wesel area. On the 4th, jets from 6. *Staffel* struck at British columns near Nordhorn and Lingen, and the next day Ar 234s joined Fw 190s and Ju 87s attacking armour in the Stolzenau and Dülmen areas. However, such was the rapidly deteriorating military position that by late on 5 April, all KG 76 personnel and aircraft at Marx were forced to evacuate, and this time they headed for Kaltenkirchen, east of the Elbe and to the north of Hamburg, which until recently had been the home of Me 262-equipped I./JG 7. As part of the relocation, one unserviceable Ar 234 had to be dismantled and its wings and fuselage loaded onto trailers to be towed for at least part of the journey by *Kettenkrad* in what must have been a tortuously slow process.

On the 6th, Ar 234s of 6./KG 76 were ordered to attack enemy tanks to the west of Achmer airfield, and on the 7th Arados from III. *Gruppe* were deployed to the east for the first time to drop bombs on forces from the Soviet 1st Ukrainian Front to the south of Berlin. However, when the jets returned to Kaltenkirchen they found the airfield being subjected to a raid by 143 B-17s of the Eighth Air Force. At least one Arado, flown by Oberleutnant Stark of 9./KG 76, landed amidst the bombing – the pilot suffered light wounds as a result. Yet, despite the bombing, the *Gruppe's* aircraft were back in the air the next day when two Ar 234s joined a formation of Fw 190s attacking enemy transport columns to the south of Hannover.

Burg was bombed on the 10th and Flieger Sturmleitner of 7./KG 76 was killed, along with a technician. As a result of the bombing, some jets were moved to the Autobahn adjacent to the airfield, from where three Ar 234s were known to have taken off, bound for Lübeck-Blankensee.

Another clash with RAF fighters took place during a bombing mission mounted by KG 76 against British troops and vehicles south of Bremen in the late afternoon of 12 April. On this occasion, Spitfire XIVs of No 41 Sqn were on patrol west of the city and had just emerged from cloud when an Ar 234 was spotted. Leading the Spitfires was Australian pilot Flt Lt Tony Gaze, who immediately jettisoned his auxiliary tank and gave chase in a dive, accompanied by Flt Lt Derek Rake. Both men claimed to have opened fire on the unfortunate jet bomber, as Gaze recalled in his combat report;

'The enemy aircraft, which was flying South, turned North and I cut the corner, closing to 800 yds. I opened fire and got strikes on the fuselage and starboard wing. I continued firing, closing slowly, and more strikes were followed by the starboard jet catching fire. I closed to 100 yds and broke away as the enemy aircraft flicked inverted after some wild jinking. It spun violently down, flicking one way and then another, and I last saw it disappear in the haze inverted at about 1,000 ft.'

Rake noted;

'As I dived towards the target I was able to position the jet within the diamond markers on the [gyro] gunsight – thus having the correct range and deflection to open fire. My opening burst hit the starboard engine and it was smoking as it rolled over and dived towards the cloud. I got in one or two more bursts as I followed it down. I believe that I claimed the "kill" but think that Tony must have had a share in finishing it off.'

Gaze and Rake claimed a 'shared' 'destroyed'.

Such was the irrefutable dominance of Allied air power over western and central Germany by mid-April 1945 that the almost continual threat or presence of fighters over the Arado bases prevented their take-offs on several occasions. However, when the jets were able to get airborne they proved effective in harassing advancing Allied forces. Twelve Ar 234s of III./KG 76 attacked vehicles southwest of Soltau on the 14th, and crossings over the Aller river were also targeted. All aircraft returned safely.

The following day, things did not go so well. Three Ar 234s from 6. *Staffel* made it into the air from Kaltenkirchen and carried out a gliding attack on enemy vehicles around Meine and against armour between Hannover and Braunschweig. Results could not be determined, and the jet flown by Leutnant Croissant was pursued by fighters, forcing the pilot to fly at low-level to the maritime base at Ratzeburg, on the shores of the Ratzeburger See south of Lübeck, where he made an interim landing. Another fighter is believed to have been the reason why Oberfeldwebel Luther crash-landed upon his return to Kaltenkirchen, the pilot being injured.

6. *Staffel* was also the subject of further emergency consolidation that day when the bulk of its personnel were reassigned to the other *Staffeln* of KG 76 and its aircraft handed over to III. *Gruppe*. The unit's remaining personnel were sent to report to the *Stab* II./KG 76 at Lauen, near Selmsdorf, east of Lübeck. Simultaneously, the *Stab* II./KG 76 was fused with the *Geschwaderstab* to form an '*Einsatzgruppe*'. It was possibly aircraft from this newly formed, ad hoc command that attacked enemy troop assembly areas around Celle and Gardelegen on the 16th. The Arados struck with effect, but smoke from the bomb blasts prevented assessment of the attack. All the jets returned safely.

Rethem, a crossing point over the Aller for Allied forces some 80 km southeast of Bremen, became the target for KG 76 over the next two days. During the afternoon of 18 April, Feldwebel Wördemann, latterly of 6. *Staffel* but now flying as part of the *Einsatzgruppe*, endured intense anti-aircraft fire and the attention of enemy fighters as he dropped a bomb from 500 m on the bridge during a weather reconnaissance flight. It was the speed of his Arado which meant he evaded the fighters, and he returned to Rethem the following day on another reconnaissance mission but was unable to make any meaningful observations. On the 19th, KG 76 sent seven Arados to bomb the pontoon at Rethem, but in the process the aircraft (F1+CA) of Oberleutnant Harald Kamrück was hit by ground fire. Although the pilot managed to release his bomb, he did not return to base.

That day, at least one Ar 234 operated over the rapidly disintegrating 'Eastern Front', but as its pilot, Major Polletin, the *Geschwader* Operations Officer, came in to land at Lübeck-Blankesee he was attacked by a Spitfire. An airfield flak gunner later recounted, 'I saw six Spitfires, in loose formation, approach the Ar 234 from behind. The Ar 234 trailed smoke and immediately went down. From my position I was unable to observe the landing or the impact.' In fact Polletin had crashed to his death in a field close to the railway line between Schönberg and Lüdersdorf.

Ar 234 V8 Wk-Nr 130008 GK+IY was fitted with four BMW 003 A-0 engines, in pairs, and was the first four-engined jet aircraft to fly. It was the inspiration for the C-series (*EN Archive*)

From 20 April through to the beginning of May, the operational emphasis for KG 76 was directed to the east, where it supported the German defensive battles around Berlin. During the evening of the 20th, a small number of jets made attacks against Soviet armour on a road leading from Zossen to Baruth/Mark, but the effects of this could not be assessed. The same day, the last elements of the *Geschwader* remaining at Alt-Lönnewitz pulled out in the face of the approaching Red Army.

A small detachment under Oberleutnant Guratzsch made its way by road to Lübeck, where it would join the *Geschwaderstab* and II./KG 76, while Hauptmann Lukesch, the *Kommandeur* of the operational training *Gruppe* III./EKG 1 formed from IV./KG 76, ensured that the last example of the small number of new, four-engined Ar 234C-3s was flown out to the relative safety of Pilsen (a small airport 85 km to the southwest of Prague) by a factory pilot. As Lukesch recalled;

'The successor to the Ar 234B-2 bomber was to have been the C-3, equipped with four BMW engines, two each in a nacelle on each wing half. It was equipped with a pressure cabin, attained a maximum horizontal speed of 950 km/h and a ceiling of 15,000 m. The gyro-steered *Bombenzielanlage* (bomb-targeting installation) was coupled with the course steering system for target-approach flight and bomb release for the course-correctable bombs. For the year 1945, a delivery of 500 aircraft of the C-series was planned, but by the end of the war only three aircraft had been delivered to IV./KG 76 (III./EKG 1). They were used for training.'

Once the C-3 had been flown out, this left just the *Gruppe's* two Me 262B-1a two-seat trainers, which were flown to Pilsen by Lukesch and Hauptmann Hans-Joachim Reymann, the *Staffelkapitän* of 11./EKG 1. It proved a difficult flight for there had been no time to prepare sufficiently, there was no radio communication and the Me 262s flew at an altitude of more than 5000 m in cloud because of icing, despite a lack of oxygen. Both aircraft reached their destination, however, where they joined the rest of III./EKG 1's personnel and a mixed bag of Ar 234B-2s and C-3s and He 111 and Si 204 trainers and transports. The latter types had been used by the *Gruppe's* pilots to evacuate vital equipment and more than 200 female auxiliary personnel. Ar 234C-3s were later photographed at Prague-Ruzyne and München-Riem at the end of the war.

Enemy motor transport to the south of Oranienburg was attacked by at least one Ar 234 from 6./KG 76 carrying an SC 500 on 24 April. Its pilot, Feldwebel Wördemann, returned to the area in the evening, where he reported bombing a pontoon bridge over the Havel.

On the 26th, having received orders to carry out 'continuous attacks' on districts of the German capital, aircraft from 6. *Staffel* operated against

Ar 234C-3 Wk-Nr 250006 was photographed at Munich-Riem shortly after the war in Europe had ended. Note the twin-jet engine nacelles, raised cockpit profile and the new style of faired periscope housing. The aircraft also had two forward-firing 20 mm MG 151 cannon installed in its nose. Diether Lukesch considered it a pleasant type to fly, but few of these rare aircraft were found by the Allies (*EN Archive*)

Ar 234B-2 Wk-Nr 140596 F1+HT of III./KG 76 (although it is believed to have been delivered initially to II. *Gruppe*), photographed at Stavanger-Sola, in Norway, in late spring/early summer 1945. This aircraft was a 'veteran', having participated in the *Einsatzstaffel*'s very first bombing mission on 23 December 1944, then taken part in the pre-strike weather reconnaissance for Operation *Bodenplatte* and in the subsequent attack on Gilze-Rijen, as well as targeting Allied troops and vehicles in the Ardennes (Leif Endsjø via Frithjof Ruud)

Soviet armour. Oberfeldwebel Breme was instructed to bomb tanks reported to be in the Tempelhof area. 'The area of Tempelhof–Neukölln–Hermannplatz is already occupied by the Russians – here you see no fires', he later recalled. 'North of the Hermannplatz, 300 m-high flames blaze in a blue sky. The Hallesches Tor is a complete sea of flames. I did not want to drop a bomb there, so I released it blind over a lake east-south-east of Schwerin.'

Three days later, Breme was back over Berlin, where he carried out an attack on columns of enemy tanks to the east of the city, while Stabsfeldwebel Karl Ballermann dropped an SD 500 in a glide attack on a specific spot in the capital's 'government district' in the afternoon. Feldwebel Wördemann also attempted to bomb the same target, but the appearance of enemy fighters forced him to drop his ordnance over Döberitz. On 2 May, two Ar 234s attacked an Allied transport column on the Autobahn near Lübeck, although by then the fighting in defence of Germany was all but over. Flights by Ar 234s had receded to mainly relocation and transfer movements, with aircraft heading northwest in an effort to avoid being caught in the vice between enemy forces approaching from the west and the east.

That day, Oberstleutnant Kowalewski ordered the *Geschwaderstab* to leave Lübeck and move north to Schleswig. It eventually settled at Taarstedt and awaited further instructions. II./KG 76, under Major Siegfried Geisler, also departed Lübeck and made its way to Schleswig, reaching the area relatively unharmed despite Allied air attacks.

Missions continued sporadically, and on 3 May eight Arados from the *Einsatzgruppe* took off from Lübeck-Blankensee to attack Red Army tanks around Berlin. Then, later that day, in what is believed to be the parting shot of KG 76, Feldwebel Drews of 8. *Staffel* bombed British vehicles south of Bremervörde in the face of dense anti-aircraft fire. However, aircraft continued to trickle in from Rechlin and other locations, including four Ar 234C-3s that arrived at Kaltenkirchen with III. *Gruppe* that day. The bulk of the *Geschwader*'s serviced Ar 234B-2s were ordered to fly to Leck, close to the Danish border. From there, on the morning of 5 May, the nine remaining flightworthy Arados of III./KG 76 led by Oberleutnant Kolm took off for

Stavanger-Sola, in Norway. They were heading north in a final attempt to evade being overrun in the hope that they could continue to mount some form of operations from an airfield still in German hands. The aircraft unable to fly out were destroyed at Leck before the arrival of the Allies.

When the German surrender finally came on 7 May, personnel from the *Geschwaderstab*, II. and III./KG 76 were grouped together in Schleswig-Holstein and later moved to internment camps within the state. On the 16th, 15.*Fliegerdivision*, evidently still functioning as a passive post-hostility command in certain respects, gave instructions for Oberstleutnant Kowalewski to report to the airfield command at Eggebek, between Flensburg and Rendsburg, where he was to be employed as commander of all flying units there, presumably in readiness for disbandment and liaison with the Allies.

To the south, those members of KG 76 and III./EKG 1 that had fled to Pilsen were subsequently moved on to Pöcking am Inn, a grass airfield 20 km southwest of Passau, where the last remaining Ar 234B-2s and C-3s were gathered. 'In the course of further retreating', recounted Diether Lukesch, 'the remaining Arados in Pöcking were destroyed by our own unit one day before the arrival of US troops.' However, it is possible a very small number of jets were flown out to Wels, in Austria, to where some personnel set out on foot and where they eventually surrendered to the Americans.

Only six Ar 234s made it to Norway, with Unteroffiziere Eckerlein and Thimm having been forced to turn around en route and land at Flensburg and Leck, respectively. Another Arado suffered engine failure and disappeared over the North Sea. Those that reached Stavanger-Sola spent five days parked in the open with other Ar 234s from the reconnaissance units 1.(F)/33, 1.(F)/123 and the *Einsatzkommando* of 1./FAGr. 1. In July a USAAF technical intelligence team led by Col Harold Watson arrived at Sola and, after assessment, took three Ar 234s including ex-III./KG 76 aircraft Wk-Nrs 140311 and 140312, the former a 'veteran' *Einsatzstaffel* machine.

The third aircraft had encountered problems, so Watson flew one of the bombers out, with former Messerschmitt test pilot *Flugkapitän Dipl.-Ing.* Karl Baur, who had been called in to assist Watson, flying the other. Watson considered the Ar 234 'a real joy to fly'. He also noted the excellent visibility, akin to 'sitting in a greenhouse'. The 'American' Arados were flown to France and eventually shipped across the Atlantic for further evaluation in the USA.

Meanwhile, the British were equally keen to get their hands on the jets. To this end, Lt Cdr Eric Brown, a Royal Navy test pilot attached to the Aerodynamics Flight (the 'Aero Flight') of the Experimental Flying Detachment at RAE Farnborough, flew Wk-Nr 140356 formerly of II./KG 76 to Farnborough. Here, it joined Wk-Nr 140173, the former F1+MT of 9./KG 76 that had been shot down at Selgersdorf on 22 February 1945 while being flown by Hauptmann Regler. Wk-Nr 140356 was flight-tested at the RAE, and the second airframe underwent detailed examination. As the first chill of a new 'Cold War' was felt, the Ar 234 and its Jumo 004 turbojets remained the cause of considerable interest to the Allies for many months to come.

APPENDICES

COLOUR PLATES COMMENTARY

1

Ar 234 V9 Wk-Nr 130009 PH+SQ, Alt-Lönnewitz, Germany, spring 1944

This aircraft, the ninth prototype, was used extensively for RATO, bomb, bomb-release and drop-tank tests at Brandenburg, Alt-Lönnewitz and Rechlin. It made more than 100 such flights, including carrying a 1000 kg bomb. Its favourable performance served to convince KG 76 *Kommodore* Oberst Storp that the Ar 234 would make an ideal high-speed bomber.

2

Ar 234B-2 Wk-Nr 140325 F1+CS of 8./KG 76 and *Einsatzstaffel*/KG 76, Handorf, Germany, November 1944

Wk-Nr 140325 was delivered to 8./KG 76 in late November 1944, but a few days later it was assigned to the *Einsatzstaffel*/KG 76. The aircraft is seen as it would typically have appeared immediately prior to a mission over the Western Front in late 1944/early 1945, with RATO units fitted and a 500 kg bomb under the fuselage.

3

Ar 234B-2 Wk-Nr 140342 F1+AS of 8./KG 76, Burg, Germany, December 1944

Wk-Nr 140342 was one of two aircraft believed to have worn the code F1+AS. This Arado first flew as NM+BP on 23 November 1944, and it was then assigned to 8./KG 76. As with several Ar 234s of KG 76, the jet also wore its individual code letter on its nose, and both the lettering and engine intake rings were in the *Staffel* colour of red.

4

Ar 234 V21 (C-3 prototype) Wk-Nr 130061, Arado Werke Brandenburg, Germany, January 1945

The V21 differentiated in profile from the twin-engined A and B variants in its revised and elevated cockpit design. This aircraft was powered by four BMW 003 engines and had provision for the installation of two rearward-firing 20 mm MG 151/20 cannon in the rear lower fuselage. Void of its *Werk Nummer* and code (RK+EK), the V21 has its prototype number applied in white just below the cockpit glazing.

5

Ar 234B-2 Wk-Nr 140173 F1+MT of 9./KG 76, Selgersdorf, Germany, February 1945

One of the most photographed Ar 234s following its forced landing at Selgersdorf after 9.*Staffelkapitän* Hauptmann Josef Regler was shot down by the P-47 flown by 1Lt David B Fox of the 366th FG on 22 February 1945, this aircraft featured a crude winter camouflage of light grey applied over the fuselage splinter pattern base, but not on the uppersurfaces. Note also that this machine had its individual letter in the *Staffel* colour of yellow applied at the top of its tail fin. The aircraft carries a 500 kg bomb for operations against Allied troops and armour, and at some point would appear to have received a replacement flap and aileron.

6

Ar 234B-2 Wk-Nr 140113 F1+AA of *Stab*(?)/KG 76, Flensburg or Schleswig, Germany, May 1945

Purported to have been an aircraft used by *Geschwaderkommodore* Oberstleutnant Robert Kowalewski towards the end of the war, Wk-Nr 140113 was finished in an earlier dark green splinter pattern of 70/71, with a replacement starboard engine unit. The aircraft carried the number '13', visible in at least one photograph, at the top of its empennage but whether this was a number that was linked to the assumed *Werk Nummer* cannot be determined for certain.

7

Ar 234B-2 Wk-Nr 140596 F1+HT of 9./KG 76, Stavanger-Sola, Norway, May 1945

Flown to Norway by Leutnant Alfred Frank in the last days of the war in Europe, F1+HT was another Ar 234 camouflaged in the variable winter scheme of pale grey, possibly 65, applied over a brown and green 81/82 base. The 'H' was in 9. *Staffel* yellow, but unlike 'M' in Profile 5, the letter was not applied to the top of the tailplane. The upper ring around the engine intake appears to be in a darker colour, possibly red, suggesting that this Jumo 004 was perhaps a replacement unit.

8

Ar 234B-2 Wk-Nr 140154 T9+IH of *Kommando Hecht*, Biblis, Germany, December 1944

Delivered to *Kommando Sperling* on 17 October 1944, this aircraft was flown on numerous western theatre sorties by Oberleutnant Erich Sommer until it was severely damaged by friendly flak on 24 December when the pilot was attempting a landing at Wiesbaden-Erbenheim. Sommer had been unable to return to Biblis – his home airfield – after it had been bombed while he was in the air. The aircraft's forward fuel tank and centre section burned out following his forced landing, although the film magazines were saved.

9

Ar 234 V7 Wk-Nr 130007 T9+MH of *Kommando Götz*, Juvincourt, France, July/August 1944

Wk-Nr 130007 became the first Ar 234 to deploy to an operational base when Oberleutnant Erich Sommer of the *Versuchsverband* OKL flew into Juvincourt, northwest of Rheims, on 25 July 1944. Sommer was duly at the controls during the first ever jet reconnaissance mission, over the Allied beachheads, on 2 August, obtaining extensive information on shipping and unloading activities. The aircraft's career was ended by a take-off accident on 1 November.

10

Ar 234B-2 Wk-Nr 140454 4U+EH of 1.(F)/123, Reinsehlen, Germany, March 1945

Probably delivered to Rheine in late January, 4U+EH was flown by Oberleutnante Krüpe, Planck and Krüger before its final flight on the early afternoon of 31 March 1945, when Oberleutnant Fritz Worschech suffered engine failure while returning to base and force-landed at Bispingen, 60 km south of Hamburg. Although Worschech survived this incident, he would be shot down and killed by Spitfire XIVs from No 350 (Belgian) Sqn on 3 May 1945.

11
Ar 234B-2 Wk-Nr 140349 T9+KH of *Kommando Sperling*, Rheine, Germany, April 1945

This aircraft was strafed by Flt Lt Dick Audet of No 411 Sqn RCAF while under tow at Rheine and claimed as an Me 262. Subsequently fitted out with dummy nacelles and cockpit framing, it appears to have been intended for use as a decoy. Images obtained by RAF photo-reconnaissance aircraft revealed its presence at the end of one runway on three different dates, and it was found in this state when the airfield was overrun by British troops on 2 April 1945.

12
Ar 234B-2 Wk-Nr 140611 T5+BH of 1.(F)/100, Lechfeld or München-Riem, Germany, April 1945

Researcher David E Brown has identified this as the Ar 234 shot down near Berchtesgaden by 2Lts Hilton O Thompson and Harold B Stotts of the 434th FS/479th FG on 25 April 1945 – the last aerial victory claimed by the Eighth Air Force. The toned-down white fuselage cross and individual aircraft letter seem to have been characteristic of 1.(F)/100's aircraft.

13
Ar 234B-2 Wk-Nr 140466 8H+HH of 1.(F)/33, Grove, Denmark, May 1945

1.(F)/33 took over coverage of southeast England and the southern part of the North Sea from March 1945. The unit was initially based at Wittmundhafen, although the progress northeastward of Allied armies compelled a move to Schleswig on 7 April. Several operations were flown from here prior to the unit's aircraft and personnel retreating to Denmark during the final days of the conflict in Europe.

14
Ar 234B-2 Wk-Nr 140142 T9+DH of *Kommando Sommer*, Udine-Campformido, Italy, April 1945

Leutnant Günther flew this aircraft from Lechfeld to Italy at the end of February 1945. He was the first of the *Kommando*'s pilots to arrive in-theatre, and operations did not commence until mid-March. On 11 April he staged through Lonate Pozzolo to cover the front from Bologna to Ancona, but was shot down by USAAF Mustangs. Injured while bailing out, he died in hospital two days later. The Arado crashed near Alfonsine, and despite German orders for its destruction, Allied Field Intelligence was able to examine it on the 19th. This is the only Ar 234 with the codes T9+DH known to have had its individual code letter repeated on the undersurface of the outer wings.

15
Ar 234B-2 Wk-Nr 140493 9V+CH of 1.(F)/5, Stavanger-Sola, Norway, February 1945

Operating from Stavanger, 1.(F)/1's remit was coverage of the east coasts of Scotland and England to identify shipping movements for the *Kriegsmarine*, which was waging its 'inshore campaign' in the North Sea with the new Type XXIII U-boats. The aircraft's codes are those of 1.(F)/5, which were retained when the unit was re-designated. The black letter C is speculative, based on the marking style 1.(F)/5 had used in 1944 for its Ju 290s.

RAF and USAAF officers examine the starboard Jumo 004 of Ar 234B-2 F1+AA of KG 76, possibly at Flensburg in May 1945. The turbojet is finished in the crude winter camouflage that appeared on a number of other Arados, suggesting that it is a replacement unit (*EN Archive*)

SELECTED BIBLIOGRAPHY AND SOURCES

Archival Sources

British National Archives, Kew, London
Air Directorate of Intelligence (AIR 40)
Air Historical Branch, RAF (AIR 20)
Air Ministry Intelligence Summaries (AIR 22)
Government Code and Cypher School (file series DEFE 3, HW 5 and HW 13)
Mediterranean Allied Air Forces (AIR 23)
Mediterranean Allied Air Forces (AIR 51)
Operations Record Books of RAF Squadrons (AIR 27)
Second Tactical Air Force (AIR 37)

Bundesarchiv–Militärarchiv, Freiburg im Breisgau
File series KART40 – Luftwaffe disposition maps
File series RL2 II and RL2 III – Luftwaffe *Führungsstab* papers
RL4 II/32 – *General der Aufklärungsflieger, Kriegstagebuch 1. Januar–26. März 1945*

Unpublished Sources

Correspondence from Oberbürgermeister a.D. Walter Carlein to Adam Thompson
Nick Beale correspondence with Erich Sommer and Werner Muffey
Theodor Rehm, *Kampfgeschwader 76 (KG 76) – Entwurf des 13. Kapitals einer Geschwadergeschichte*, Augsburg, undated (via Eddie J Creek)
Various reports, notes and tabular data prepared and/or kept by the *Einsatzstaffel* (9./KG 76) and III./KG 76 (from collection of Eddie J Creek)

Books

Bauduin, Philippe and Charon, Eric, *Normandie 44—Le Photos de l'Avion Espion*, Éditions Mait' Jacques, 1997
Brown, David E, Tomás Poruba and Jan Vladar, *Messerschmitt Me 262 Production and Arado Ar 234 Final Operations*, JaPo, 2012
Kaiser, Jochen, *Die Ritterkreuzträger der Kampfflieger, Band 1*, Luftfahrtverlag Start, 2010
Kaiser, Jochen, *Die Ritterkreuzträger der Kampfflieger, Band 2*, Luftfahrtverlag Start, 2011
Koos, Volker, *Arado Flugzeugwerke 1925–1945*, HEEL Verlag, 2007
Kranzhoff, Jörg Armin, *Arado – History of an Aircraft Company*, Schiffer Publishing, 1997
Ruud, Frithjof, *Profiles in Norway No 5, Arado Ar 234 B-2*, Arild Kjæraas, 2006
Shores, Christopher and Thomas, Chris, *2nd Tactical Air Force, Volume Three, From the Rhine to Victory, January to May 1945*, Classic Publications, 2006
Smith, J Richard and Creek, Eddie J, *Arado 234 Blitz*, Monogram Aviation Publications, 1992
Smith, J Richard and Creek, Eddie J, *On Special Missions*, Classic Publications, 2003
Sommer, Erich, (ed. J Richard Smith), *Luftwaffe Eagle – A WWII German Airman's Story*, Grub Street, 2018

INDEX

Page numbers in **bold** refer to illustrations and their captions.